Rat River Trapper

Who was the strange loner that roamed the
wastes of the Yukon in the late 1920s, with
a smoking rifle in his hands? Indians fled at
the sight of him, Mounties fell before him.
The Eskimos called him "the man who steals
gold from men's teeth". The press referred to
him as "the mad trapper" and "the toughest
customer ever encountered by the R.C.M.P."
He used the name of Albert Johnson, but who
he really was remains a mystery to this day —
decades after the Mounties finally cornered
and killed him at a bend in the Rat River on
February 17, 1932. . . . Thomas P. Kelley is the
author of numerous articles and stories and of
several books, including *The Black Donnellys*,
a perennial best-seller which has been read by
hundreds of thousands since it first appeared
in 1954, and *Run Indian Run*, another Paper-
Jacks true adventure story set in the Canadian
North.

Rat River Trapper

Rat River Trapper

The Story of Albert Johnson, the Mad Trapper

Thomas P. Kelley

PaperJacks

A division of General Publishing Co. Limited

First published by PaperJacks
A division of General Publishing Co. Limited,
30 Lesmill Road, Don Mills, Ontario

ISBN 0-7737-7004-6

Printed and bound in Canada

Rat River Trapper

CHAPTER ONE

I arrived in Yukon Territory –
That grim land of ice, wind and snow.
Men called me the Rat River Trapper.
My story is one you should know.

Late in the afternoon of August 21, 1927, the man with the hungry gun arrived at the small Canadian settlement of Ross River Post in Yukon Territory. So began one of the strangest stories in the history of the Arctic.

In time, that story became a legend destined to be told and retold down through the years, when elders of the Northland gathered around cabin lamps as the snow piled high to the windows — a legend that will continue to be heard through years to come. It is a true story, remember. A true story of howling huskies, dangerous trails, and desolate tundra in a frozen world across which a fugitive flees before oncoming posses. Exchanges of rifle fire and hoarse shouts are heard, uniformed Mounties gasp and fall, and the snow is reddened, while Arctic winds cut like icy sabres in a temperature hovering at 55 degrees below.

A deadly game of hide-and-seek went on for days, then weeks, in the glow of the Northern Lights, as posse members wondered if they would live to see tomorrow and telegraph wires crackled out the latest developments of the chase through the frozen ether.

The stranger who walked into the isolated settlement of Ross River Post was Albert Johnson, destined to be known as the Rat River Trapper. His origins were a mystery at the time and have remained so even to this day. His unbelievable exploits were to appear in headlines throughout North America, where they thrilled the millions who read of him and waited for the next edition paper as they speculated on what was to follow. And plenty did. The Rat River Trapper not only brought about a one-man reign of terror as well as death to two officers of the Royal Canadian Mounted Police. He also made the police look foolish, outshot them again and again, and single-handed carried on what came to be called the Arctic Circle War.

The purpose of this volume is to tell the story of his war, a series of cold confrontations and bloody combats that involved one man against the mankind he hated. A man who explained his reason for slaughtering his fellow humans with three words: "Gnats breed lice."

However, as usually is the case at the beginning of any history-making event, no one sensed as much, and the arrival of Albert Johnson at that small outpost on the rim of the Arctic aroused little interest. This was to be expected; a new face was nothing unusual in the area. Wandering prospectors and trappers would occasionally appear at Ross River Post, where they would remain for a few days, secure supplies, then drift on, and the stranger was regarded as but another member of that restless race of northern nomads.

The few inhabitants who bothered to give the newcomer a passing glance saw a man in his early thirties with stern, swarthy features—a man of above average height, whose weight had been hardened to steel-like sinew by years of trail travel and constant exertion in the open. He was dressed in the usual dark and coarse apparel of the trapper, with a battered cap covering his thick brown hair.

His pack was strapped to his shoulders, and in his right hand Albert Johnson carried a high-powered 99 Savage .30-30 rifle—"the hungry gun".

His presence did attract the attention of a trapper named Jake Niddery, who spoke of it on a number of occasions later. Niddery, who was a familiar figure in the territory at the time and died in Northern Ontario only a few years ago, would tell the following story:

"I happened to be on the street that day, large as life, when Albert Johnson arrived at Ross River Post. Of course, at the time I had no idea as to who he was or where he came from. To me, he appeared to be but another roving trapper, and it is just as well that I did not know him for what he really was. If I had, I would have probably made tracks and still be running.

"As I recall, it was late in the afternoon and I stood before Taylor and Drury's trading store, trying to get my pipe going, when I saw the stranger coming towards me with a long-strided walk. And I remember saying to myself: 'Here comes a fellow I wouldn't like to tangle with. I'll bet he hasn't smiled in twenty years, and is mean enough to throw stones at his grandmother.'

"Then I sure got a surprise. For, as I stood there watching, a puppy appeared from somewhere, ran forward barking, and stopped at the stranger's feet. And would you believe it? Why, that fellow, who looked as though he had about as much human kindness in him as you would find in a falling ax, stopped to pat and scratch the young pup's back before he went on. And I couldn't help but think, I'd seen it with my own eyes, and it goes to prove how wrong you can be when you first size up a fellow man. For all his hard appearance, that stranger likes animals, and in my book it means he can't be a hundred percent bad. He has to have a heart somewhere."

It could have been that Albert Johnson was not a hundred percent bad. Very few people are. But the days were not far distant when mothers in the frozen Northland would silence their unruly children with, "Hush, or the Rat River Trapper will get you!"

With the setting sun a giant bonfire in the west, Albert Johnson walked past the weather-beaten structures of Ross River Post. He neither paused nor made inquiries. In his case, this was understandable, as it would have meant conversing with a fellow human. Something that Johnson loathed and only did as a last resort.

Instead, having traversed the length of the little settlement, he continued to go forward, with his course paralleling the Ross River less than fifty yards to the north. Overhead, evening clouds were sculptured in the sky.

It was not until he was nearly a mile beyond Ross River Post that Albert Johnson halted, at a cluster of trees with a clearing in the centre. The trees stretched on until they were close to the bank of the river. A look of interest lightened his grim features. Ah, this was it — the ideal spot for what he had in mind. He would take over this handy cove. The thought of any right of ownership did not disturb him. If some headstrong fool came along and ordered him to be on his way, he could handle that. To Albert Johnson's way of thinking, possession was not merely nine-tenths of the law. It was ten-tenths.

Thus he confidently entered the clearing in that cluster of trees, removed the heavy pack from his shoulders, and with a skill that told of long practice set up camp within sound of the flowing river. Best of all, to his way of thinking, he was alone. Once more he knew the glorious silence of the solitude he always craved. He inhaled deeply to fill his lungs with the crisp Arctic air. Again he could play his favourite role of a lone Adam in a world devoid of any other human life — a role that fitted Albert Johnson like a glove.

That night a campfire gleamed among the trees while the aroma of frying bacon was wafted on the air. Later, beneath a star-studded sky, Albert Johnson sat quietly before his campfire and gazed into its glow. Just what his thoughts were, no one will ever know, though the hour was getting on and his campfire was dying before he finally rolled up in his sleeping blanket.

First, however, as had long been his nightly custom, Albert Johnson, who neither smoked nor drank and rarely used profanity, sank to his knees and prayed to his Maker.

CHAPTER TWO

The Indians in that Arctic wasteland,
Would run from me with frightened cries.
They all feared the Rat River Trapper,
And said they saw death in my eyes.

The Indians of the far north, who seemed immune to fear as they battled its perils and hardships, were known to wheel and flee at the approach of the Rat River Trapper. Either that, or crouch low in hiding till he had continued on his way. Today, in the files of the Royal Canadian Mounted Police, can be found this report: "The Indians living in the territory were visibly afraid of Albert Johnson. In fact, they would have absolutely nothing to do with him."

On the morning following his encampment among the trees, Albert Johnson returned to Ross River Post. Two decades earlier, some pioneer wit had described the territory as being "a land of eleven months' winter and one month of poor sleighing, fit only for Eskimoes and fools". However, as it was the month of August at the time of Johnson's arrival, Ross River Post was enjoying a few weeks of comparative warmth and sunshine before the giant snowflakes would again swirl earthward in their tireless struggle to obliterate all evidence of human existence.

He directed his footsteps towards the trading store of Taylor and Drury.

On the day in question, August 22, 1927, clerk Roy Buttle was behind the counter of the store. A man in his late thirties and a popular figure at Ross River Post, Buttle had spent a number of years in the north, and was known for fairness in all his dealings. On a near-by chair sat the Swedish-born trapper, Otto Paulson, who had dropped in to the store for a chat with Buttle and was apparently a very observant individual. Paulson was to reminisce in later years:

"I have seen the Rat River Trapper. I heard his quiet voice, and I had the same creepy sensation as everybody else when he looked at me with those green eyes. His eyes seemed to be always asking questions and he somehow made the air feel sticky, while you got to thinking that you could hear the sound of shovels digging your grave. That's the way he affected you.

"It was back in August of 1927. One morning I was sitting in the trading store at Ross River Post, chewing the fat with Roy Buttle—I'd known him for years. Suddenly the small bell above the door rang and there he stood in the doorway.

"Yes, there he was, less than ten feet from me, and I got an uncomfortable feeling right away. As though someone had poured a glass of ice-water down my back. No, I did not know who he was then. I knew the men he shot, though. Every one of them was a good friend of mine."

Clerk Roy Buttle came forward with his best professional manner.

"Welcome, stranger. You are new to this district, as I have never seen you before. Where are you from?"

Albert Johnson broke a two months' silence with a one-word answer: "Nowhere."

Such a brief reply was typical. He was never known to either laugh or smile, and usually guarded his words with miserly caution. True, there are two known occasions when he permitted himself the luxury of a conversation, but in most cases Albert Johnson was about as communicative as a sphinx and spoke only when the situation made it necessary. Even then, his responses were usually limited to an abrupt yes or no.

Old-timers throughout the Northwest Territories who actually saw Albert Johnson usually tell of his almost constant silence, and invariably agree on one point: he had a habit of shooting backward glances over his shoulder, as though expecting an attack from some lurking enemy.

As for Roy Buttle, his years behind the counter catering to various whims and wishes had taught him diplomacy. So he gave one of his ready smiles.

"I have never been to Nowhere. Now what can I do for you?"

The reply of the other was to produce a folded sheet of paper from the pocket of his dark-blue shirt and wordlessly hand it to Buttle. It was a written list of supplies—quantities of tea, flour, bacon, sugar, beans, and other items—that would be his mainstay during the months of isolation ahead. His rifle would supply whatever else was needed.

"I can see him now, as he stood there, waiting for me to fill my order," Buttle later said. "Stone-faced. Tough. Muscular. Must have been close to the six-foot mark. And he—well, somehow he awed you, and you damn well knew that he was not the kind of a man to take liberties with. That he was as dangerous as a dynamite keg that only needed a match to light it. So you kept your distance and hoped he would soon be on his way.

"But what stands out in my memory of the man were those green eyes, like green ice, constantly shooting around the store. First they would shoot to Paulson, then to me. Next they would go to the ceiling, drop to the floor, then sweep along the merchandise on the counter and the shelves behind me. As though he was taking inventory, and if there had been flies in the place I'll wager he would have counted them. And he kept looking over his shoulder."

With a speed taught by experience, Roy Buttle soon had the ordered provisions wrapped and piled on the counter, after which they were placed in two burlap bags produced for the purpose. There had been but one pause in the entire procedure. Buttle, scanning the list the stranger had handed him, had come upon an entry that caused him to raise his eyes.

"It says here that you want six boxes of kidney pills. Are you sure it's what you mean? That you need that many? Six boxes?"

Albert Johnson frowned slightly and nodded.

His continual need for pills is one of the few facts actually known about his physical welfare. Though the man's existence was practically a total mystery prior to his appearance at Ross River Post in 1927, Robert Levac of the trading post at Fraser Falls, Archie Currie of Binet's Store at Mayo, and John Saunders of Fort McPherson all told later how they had, at one time or other, sold quantities of kidney pills to "a stranger who rarely spoke and had green eyes".

"There it is, your order as you asked for it, stranger. It comes to exactly forty-nine dollars and twenty cents. Do you think you can carry both bags with you, or do you want to come back for one of them?"

The response of the other was to make history in the small settlement of Ross River Post, as well as create a mystery that has never been solved. For his right hand went to his hip-pocket, and with a somewhat bored nonchalance, he withdrew an enormous roll of banknotes. Tens, twenties and hundreds. A roll of banknotes which, according to the joint opinion of Buttle and Paulson, "was big enough to choke a horse and must have contained at least three thousand dollars". Startled whistles broke from the lips of both of them. But if what they had seen surprised them, what followed must have been brain-reeling.

After contemplating that thick wad of currency for several seconds, Albert Johnson put it back and from his left hip-pocket brought forth another roll of bills that equalled the size of the first. As Buttle and Paulson looked on wide-eyed, he dropped a fifty-dollar bill on the counter, after which that bundle of what is said to be the root of all evil was returned to the left hip-pocket.

From what source did Albert Johnson receive his seemingly endless supply of money? The answer to that question has long been a matter of speculation on the part of certain American as well as Canadian officials.

It is known that from 1927 to 1932, whenever he appeared at remote trading posts the roving Albert Johnson—he was apparently forever on the move—always had huge sums of money in his possession, and he is said to have occasionally displayed large American banknotes. This, possibly, led to the rumour that he was in reality an embittered American millionaire who had been jilted by his fiancee and who, instead of following the accepted pattern and becoming a soldier of the Foreign Legion on the hot sands of the Sahara, had chosen to spend his life wandering over the dreary regions around the rim of the Arctic.

Another rumor was that Albert Johnson, under another name, was actually a notorious Chicago gangster who had escaped to northern Canada by plane, following the successful holdup of an armoured car; furthermore, that he had brought his ill-gotten gains, totalling around a half-million dollars, with him, and was only staying in the north country "till the heat blew off" in his native land. However, that theory could not explain why most of his money was in Canadian funds.

But one thing is certain. For years, though his visible income was apparently nil, he always carried an abundant supply of currency with him wherever he went. And he made no pretence at concealing it.

But to return to the trading store at Ross River Post, Yukon Territory, in August 1927:

Roy Buttle placed the banknote in the cash drawer, deducted the forty-nine dollars and twenty cents, and laid the eighty cents' change on the counter. Otto Paulson was to tell of what followed:

"Then Johnson grabbed one of the burlap bags that held his supplies, swung it over his shoulder, and seemed to forget about his change. He was just going to pick up the other bag when in dashed two Indian boys about seven years old. Somehow, they had either found or been given a nickel, and they charged over to the candy case—you know, gumdrops and peppermint bull's-eyes.

"Now, some of them Yukon Indians, as you probably know, are not the cleanest people in the world, and both of the lads smelled like wet goats.

"As for the stranger, he watched them, and then he turned to Roy Buttle. He pointed to the silver on the counter, then to the youngsters, then to the candy case, and his meaning was noonday clear. He wanted Buttle to take the money and treat the kids to a feast of candy. Buttle nodded to indicate that he understood what was expected of him.

"With that he swung the other bag on his shoulder and took his departure. I stepped forward and opened the door for him. He just gave a nod of thanks and went out without another word. It just goes to show, doesn't it?"

Paulson was not the sort of man to withhold information from the public, and by sundown the entire populace of Ross River Post was aware of the presence of a stranger who carried a fortune in banknotes. Facts were soon exaggerated, as they frequently are in such cases, and before the clock had ticked off another twenty-four hours it was common knowledge throughout the settlement that a millionaire was encamped but a short distance away among a cluster of trees that led down to the river.

A millionaire who frowned on all intruders. Furthermore, he appeared to be a man who was able to handle himself and his rifle, and any would-be thief should think twice before taking on something he might regret.

At that time, Corporal Claude Tidd of the Royal Canadian Mounted Police was stationed at Ross River Post, and it was agreed by the inhabitants that he was just the man to handle the mystery of the green-eyed Rockefeller encamped so close to the settlement. But, as luck would have it, Corporal Tidd was on patrol duty, up the Pelly River, and was not expected to return for at least a week. Meanwhile, there appeared to be no immediate solution to the quandary.

Several days passed that were marked by a hum of activity in the encampment among the trees. A great deal of hammering and sawing could be heard—a din that began early in the morning, and lasted throughout most of the daylight hours—which definitely suggested that the stranger was up to something. Just what it was, however, remained a mystery, as the locals of the settlement were hesitant to go out to the woods and investigate. Otto Paulson had muttered that the stranger had "a look of death in his eyes", and already rumours were being heard of how the Indians would make themselves scarce at the sight of the man.

So the none-too-courageous inhabitants decided to wait till the return of Corporal Tidd to confront the stranger and demand an explanation for his presence. It was the only sensible thing to do, wasn't it? And, needless to add, from the point of view of self-protection it was the safest thing to do. Ah, yes. Before setting out on any venture that might involve danger, it is best to have a husky uniformed Mountie go on ahead, investigate the hazards, and pull your chestnuts out of the fire for you.

Actually, the cause of the din that resounded from the trees was Albert Johnson building a boat.

A boat, he hoped, that would carry him and his supplies far up the Ross River, then on through the Stewart and the Rogue rivers till he finally reached the isolation that lay beyond. Only then, in some uncharted and forgotten wilderness where man did not go, would he find true peace. This patch of woods near the river would indeed be the ideal spot to launch his newly constructed craft.

Then came the afternoon when Corporal Tidd returned to Ross River Post, his patrol of the Pelly River completed, and he scarcely had time to reach his quarters before he heard of the stranger in the woods. The righteous matrons came forward first to voice their suspicions of the newcomer, while their men nodded in agreement. Something had to be done.

Then Paulson called on the Mountie: "The stranger has money to burn, I tell you. Furthermore, he doesn't give a damn who knows it. He's that sure of himself. He realizes that a man will think twice before tackling him."

All this, Tidd well knew, was the direct opposite of the behaviour of most of the wanderers who travelled around the Yukon. Invariably they were hard-pressed for cash. How was it, then, that the newcomer was so well supplied? Again, just who was he and where did he come from? His curiosity aroused, Tidd that same evening walked out to the near-by woods to question the stranger, only to find that he was too late.

Early that very morning, August 29, 1927, Albert Johnson had taken his departure and sailed up the Ross River.

So the two men never did meet. There was no conversation in the woods that evening, and Albert Johnson was not obliged to hear a lot of questions that might have annoyed him. And thus—perhaps— did Corporal Tidd miss the honour of being the first Mountie to be shot down by the Rat River Trapper.

CHAPTER THREE

On a raft, I sailed down the Peel River.
Then spoke words that proved to be true,
When I told brave Millen of the Mounties:
"I've a bullet I'm saving for you."

"Damn the women of today. Always jumping into bed with this man or that man. They're like bitches in heat."

According to a story that was told of him, Albert Johnson shouted the above scorching denunciation somewhere near the south fork of the Stewart River before an audience of three prospectors. Around noon on a day in the early fall of 1929, the roving Rat River Trapper had stumbled upon their encampment and accepted their offer of a meal. Then one of them, reading aloud from a month-old newspaper, informed the group of the ever-increasing birth rate throughout the world.

Briefly, statistics proved the population of our planet to be a bit over 2,000,000,000 people. This, in turn, gave an average density of forty-five people per square mile of the world's land area, excluding Antarctica and uninhabited islands. Each day, more than 130,000 babies were being born and the world's population would soon double. It was expected to reach nearly 7,000,000,000 by the year 2000. The article concluded with the fanciful calculation that, if the population increase continued unabated for the next five hundred years, there would be but one yard of land on earth for each person. Strictly a case of standing room only.

The reader finally laid down his paper with a laugh.

"What do you think of that, stranger? Something to mull over eh? A hundred and thirty thousand babies are being born every day, or nearly a million of them a week. Why, soon all you will see up here is a mass of humanity, with folks running into each other. Yes, and in time there will be so many people in the world that they'll have to stand on each other's heads."

The solitude-loving Albert Johnson is said to have leapt to his feet, raised a clenched fist above his head, shouted out his unflattering comment on modern women, and immediately followed up with:

"Kids, kids. Always kids who will raise more kids. The only way to be free from the stink of humanity is to go to the moon."

"But there have always been children since the first pair in the garden, and there always will be," put in one of the men.

"That's right," spoke up another. "Down through the ages to come, men and women will continue to mate and multiply. It was meant to be that way, and there is nothing that can change it."

"Yes there is. A long, sharp knife can change it," snapped Albert Johnson. "A keen steel blade in experienced hands can damn soon take the steam out of sex, and in time will whittle the world's population down to one. Which is just what it should be."

With that, he threw the tin plate that contained his proffered meal to the ground, swung his heavy pack to his shoulders, and reached for his rifle. Then, without as much as a look at the three men, he walked rapidly away and soon disappeared from view. Then and only then did one of the prospectors break the silence.

"Boys, I don't know who that fellow was, but he sure has little love for the rest of us who walk the earth today."

As was mentioned earlier, prior to his appearance at Ross River Post in 1927, little or nothing backed by positive proof is known of Albert Johnson. It is estimated that he was about thirty years of age at the time, but to get him to divulge any information about himself was like trying to learn the secrets of life eternal from a stone Buddha.

One matter is certain: he had no criminal record in North America. After his death, fingerprints were taken from his corpse and sent to both Ottawa and Washington, in the hope that they might establish some identification. But the fingerprints could not be linked to anyone with a criminal record in either country.

Of course there are the inevitable stories that have been told through the years, and can still be heard in the Northland.

One of these stories seems to be at odds with his otherwise abstemious way of life. A man answering Johnson's description, who called himself Al Johnson and wore a large diamond ring, spent several weeks in Nome, Alaska, back in 1924; he is said to have promptly departed after shooting and killing a gambler during a poker game.

Then there is the report of R.C.M.P. Corporal Arthur Thornthwaite, that he had talked to a man who claimed to have known Johnson, years earlier, in Dawson.

There was also a rumour that appears to have been totally baseless: that Albert Johnson was an escaped convict from a chain-gang in some southern state, where he had been serving a life sentence for murder. Equally ridiculous would seem to be the story that he had once been a member of a crew that had sailed to the tip of Ellesmere Island, where Johnson displayed his uncanny marksmanship with a rifle by shooting, from the ship's deck, the Arctic wolves running along the shore.

However, of all the stories told of personal contact with Albert Johnson, the experiences related by trapper George Case are not only unique, they might even contain more truth than has come from any other source.

"In all, I knew Albert Johnson for nearly eight years, as fate had a habit of throwing us together from time to time. And for some strange reason, I believe I am the only man in the world that he could even tolerate. Who knows, it could have been because I never asked too many questions or pressed him for information about himself. Yet, even then, he could only take me in small doses. After a few minutes together he would just get up and leave—as though a little of me went a long way.

"But I would like to make it quite clear that the stories told about him being mad or bush crazy are dead wrong. He knew a hell of a lot about things like astronomy and he spoke like a man with education—that is, when he would speak at all, which was not very often."

Trapper Case also told how, with the passing of the years, he eventually learned that Albert Johnson was an American, born in North Dakota, and that in his twenty-second year he had inherited a fortune from an uncle.

According to Case, his meetings with Johnson were usually unexpected. Like the last time their paths crossed, one night in February 1932, in a snowbound cabin less than two hundred miles from the Alaska border.

"Of course, at that time Johnson had already shot down King and Millen, and every man in the Arctic was gunning for him. Inspector Eames was on the radio from Aklavik asking for volunteers for the hunt and warning them how dangerous it was.

"And damn it, the men he shot down, a lot of us knew them and they were regarded pretty highly.

"They had even brought in that bush pilot, Wop May, from Fort McMurray—that's a thousand miles away—to track him from the air, and he carried dynamite with him just in case. The odds looked to be about ten thousand to one against Johnson.

"But on that last night, out of the blue he came to my cabin, and he must have known that they'd be getting him any day. But he didn't seem worried—almost like he wasn't interested. But then I'd never known him to be afraid of anything. Anything!

" 'My rifle will take care of me,' he said. 'It always has, always will. And I'll die of old age with my boots off. As for the posses, the Mountie has yet to be born that I can't outshoot. Yes, and they all damn well know it.' "

It was on August 29, 1927, that Albert Johnson had taken his departure from Ross River Post. Then a

year passed, during which time his whereabouts were
a matter of speculation, though it would seem likely,
as later developments indicated, that he spent a
number of months in the wild territory around the
head of the Ross River.

Of course, it could have been sheer coincidence,
but the fact remains that right about that time a
roving prospector is known to have entered the same
district and was never seen again. Nor could any
evidence be discovered that he had been a victim of
foul play. He entered the territory, vanished, and that
was it. Years later, an Indian who had met and talked
with the prospector just a few days prior to the
latter's disappearance provided this description:

"He was a short, jolly man with a black beard, and
when he laughed you could see the gold in his teeth."

At the time of Albert Johnson's death, no fewer
than seven pieces of gold dental work were found in
his possession, although his own teeth were in perfect
condition. The discovery caused considerably comment, the opinion of many being that the Rat River
Trapper had been a mass murderer with an insane
craving for the gold dental pieces he pulled from the
mouths of his victims.

It was not until August 1928 that the records again
picked up the trail of the wandering Albert Johnson,
when he arrived at the trading store of Robert Levac
at Fraser Falls, Yukon Territory. Levac later said that
the man came at sundown, carrying an unusually
heavy and bulky trail-pack, and said his name was
Albert Johnson. He also had with him his rifle and a
number of marten skins.

"He asked if I could put him up for a few days,
and I told him I had a cabin behind the store. Despite

my protests, he insisted on paying for the use of it and shoved a twenty-dollar bill into my hand."

Four days passed, during which, according to Levac, Albert Johnson spent most of the time in the cabin, lying on the bunk and staring at the ceiling. Occasionally he would walk over to the store and buy something to eat, but he would make a quick departure and it was evident that he wanted to be alone. He seemed moody and irritable. Would frown, shake his head, and turn away if someone sought to engage him in the most trivial conversation.

"When he would come to the store," Levac recalled, "I noticed that he had a habit of casting glances over his shoulders. Once he did say something about having built a boat and then later wrecking it up the Ross River."

On the morning of the fifth day Levac went to the cabin to make a bid on the marten pelts, only to discover that Albert Johnson had vanished. Some time during the previous night, silently and unseen, the Rat River Trapper had left Fraser Falls, and he never returned to that district again.

It is known that a few days later—on August 29, 1928, to be exact—Albert Johnson arrived at the settlement of Mayo, Yukon Territory.

It would appear that, as usual, he was anxious to get away from civilization and return to his beloved wilderness. Certainly, what followed indicated as much, for he went directly to the trading store managed by W. H. Jeffrey and disposed of his marten pelts for the sum of $680. Since the trading store did not have the necessary cash on hand, the transaction had to be completed on the following day, when Albert Johnson presented their cheque at the Bank of

Montreal. And you cannot help but wonder if, somewhere in some musty record file, there might be a cheque bearing the Rat River Trapper's endorsement. If so, it is probably the only example of his signature in existence.

Johnson tarried in Mayo just long enough to purchase supplies from Binet's Trading Store, including six boxes of kidney pills. The clerk on duty at the time, Archie Currie, later described something silent and sinister about the man.

"He did nothing wrong, he said nothing wrong. In fact, he never opened his mouth. Just handed me a list of the supplies he needed, then paid for them and went. But there was something about the man that gave me the creeps, and I felt relieved when he left the store."

In later years, a story was to be told about an incident which occurred that day in Mayo.

According to this tale, four or five idlers were killing time before the store just as Johnson came out. One of them was extolling the ability of the police in keeping law and order throughout the Yukon.

"They are all good men, but my pick of the lot is Staff Sergeant Hersey, Edgar Millen, and Bunce King. No man ever walked in shoe leather that those three can't take care of, even if they have to go to the ends of the world to get him."

As the speaker finished, so the story goes, Albert Johnson glanced at him, then walked away from the store and up the street.

That is the story. One so trivial it would not have been set down here except for its surprising aftermath.

Admittedly, Hersey, Millen, and King were three brave and capable officers of the law. They had proved as much, time and again. But the speaker had said that no man ever walked that they could not cope with and capture. Now, that statement was false. There was one such man—as time would prove.

CHAPTER FOUR

Eskimoes in Northwest Territories
Upon me a title bequeathed,
For they spoke of the Rat River Trapper
as "the man who steals gold from men's teeth".

Canada's Northwest Territories is a remote world of
snow and isolation, an almost unbelievable vastness
totalling more than a million square miles. It is there
that the Eskimoes, as their ancestors for generations
before them, hunt for fur-bearing animals.

The territories do not stop at the shores of the
Arctic Ocean. Far, far to the north lies Ellesmere
Island, a land so bleak that even the Eskimoes found
it impossible to live there and abandoned it centuries
ago.

But life does exist on Ellesmere Island today. On
the northern tip of the island is Alert, where there is a
weather station and a Canadian Armed Forces base.
Even there the name of Albert Johnson is not
unknown.

Recently a serviceman who had completed his tour
of duty on Ellesmere told me:

"It was at Alert that I first heard stories of Albert
Johnson, the Rat River Trapper. An Eskimo who
worked in one of the kitchens claimed that his father

had seen the man around Baker Lake in the North-west Territories, and said that the Eskimoes used to speak of Johnson as 'the man who steals gold from men's teeth'."

In the north-west section of the Northwest Territories mainland is Aklavik. It was from there that the outside world first became aware of the beginning of the 48-day Arctic Circle War. It was not far from there that the war began.

Today, eighty miles south of Aklavik on a bluff overlooking the swift-moving Rat River, can be seen the crumbling ruins of what was once a small cabin. Trappers and Indians occasionally pass by, and some-times stop to gaze at that lonely spot, while birds wing high overhead and cold winds tell of oncoming winter. For it was there that Albert Johnson shot down his first Mountie.

Only a few miles down the river from the ruins of that cabin is a river junction that has witnessed sheer hell in bygone days.

Wild and desolate is that point where the swirling Rat River foams and rushes into Driftwood Creek, some eighty-five miles from Aklavik. Seemingly accursed, it is one of the most dismal spots on God's earth. Even before the turn of the century that junction had been dolefully named Destruction City.

Back in the gold-rush days, many adventurers hurrying on to the Klondike with high hopes of a fast fortune saw their dreams vanish in that area, for it is there that the Rat River is marked by a series of rapids so treacherous they have lined the banks with the wreckage of boats, rafts, and equipment. In the bitter winter of 1898, four men died of scurvy at the river junction while waiting helplessly for a break in the weather before pushing on to the gold fields.

Then, in the summer of 1907, another gruesome discovery. A half-mile from the junction, two hunters came upon the bleaching bones of Old Cuddy, a trapper whose whereabouts had been unknown for a year. He had apparently stepped into his own bear trap, and then known a lingering and painful death, his imprisoned left leg making him a helpless victim of the elements and the wolves.

So, all in all, "Destruction City" seems a quite appropriate name.

In the files of the Royal Canadian Mounted Police is the following:

"On July 9, 1931, a stranger arrived at Fort McPherson, Northwest Territories, under rather unusual circumstances. This man drifted down the Peel River from the direction of the Yukon Territory on a raft consisting of three large logs, to a spot about three miles above Fort McPherson. There he abandoned his crude craft and, apparently with either little or no outfit, walked the remainder of the way into the Fort where he purchased supplies. He was said to be well stocked with cash."

There is no record of Albert Johnson ever being otherwise.

True, he was minus his heavy trail-pack, and his clothing was much the worse for wear. Just what had happened to reduce him to such a predicament was never learned, but it must have been something hectic.

In fact, from the time he left Mayo nearly three years earlier till he reached Fort McPherson, very little is known of Albert Johnson's movements. We have only legends to go on, some of which hint that he spent considerable time in the Yukon Territory, trapping in the Macmillan River district between Mayo and Ross River Post.

John Zimmerlee, who operated a trading store at Russel Creek, claimed that Albert Johnson bought supplies from him on two occasions, and that once he purchased some rifle shells. A trapper named Fredrickson of the Russel Post area said that he once sold a canoe to Albert Johnson, and Indians later found it abandoned in the upper waters of the Macmillan River.

However, when Albert Johnson arrived in Fort McPherson on July 9, 1931, despite his tattered apparel and lack of equipment, along with the bank-rolls that bulged his hip-pockets he also brought his inevitable companion—his high-powered 99 Savage 30-30 rifle.

In Fort McPherson he rented a cabin where he remained for twelve days. The owner of the cabin, Jess Clifford, later said:

"Several times I dropped in to see how he was making out. But he rarely spoke. Just nodded or shook his head when I asked him anything. He seemed to be always thinking. Thinking. He spent most of his time lying in his bunk and looking at the ceiling."

But he did not spend all his time thus. While in Fort McPherson, Albert Johnson bought an entire new outfit. He also purchased an unusual quantity of supplies, as well as a new and large canoe. As for ammunition, it was said that "he bought enough to fight an army". To the local inhabitants, wise to the ways of a trapper, it was evident that the newcomer planned to travel either up or down the Peel River, and then go inland to some remote spot for a considerable length of time.

In the process of outfitting, Albert Johnson spent money so freely at the Northern Traders Limited and the Hudson's Bay Company that people began to talk. So much so, in fact, that rumours of the stranger in Fort McPherson who tossed money around recklessly soon reached the police detachment at nearby Arctic Red River. It resulted in Constable Edgar Millen, an experienced and tactful officer, being dispatched to Fort McPherson to question the man.

Millen had no trouble in locating the object of his search. Jess Clifford took him to the cabin where the stranger was staying. Lying on his bunk, Albert Johnson sent a casual glance towards the two men as they entered. Then Millen came forward.

"I am Constable Edgar Millen of the Royal Canadian Mounted Police, and I am here to ask you a few questions. First, what is your name?"

There was no immediate answer, and a silence followed. From his bunk, with hands clasped over his head, Albert Johnson continued to send a calm and somewhat bored gaze towards his uniformed visitor. More silence. Then finally Millen spoke again:

"I would like to know your name, sir."

"Albert Johnson."

"I understand you plan to do some trapping around here, Mr. Johnson," continued Millen. "Of course, as you know, you will need a licence. Do you have one?"

Albert Johnson shook his head.

"Then I would suggest that you secure one as soon as possible," advised the other. "You can get a licence at Aklavik—or, for that matter, at Arctic Red River, which is much closer."

During his twenty-minute stay at the cabin, Millen gained little information from Albert Johnson, other than that the man had considered the possibility of going over the Rat River portage. Millen sensed that he preferred the wilderness to any association with humanity. However, since there was nothing of a criminal nature about such a tendency, and he had not, to the best of the constable's knowledge, broken any law, Millen finally took his departure. When he reached the door, Edgar Millen is said to have spoken the words:

"Good-bye for now. I am occasionally on patrol duty in the Rat River district, and, who knows?—we may meet again some day."

Jess Clifford reported later that Albert Johnson, who still lay on his bunk and whose eyes had never left the constable, replied with a quiet:

"I'll be looking forward to that meeting."

Some six months later, on January 30, 1932, five miles south of a creek that empties into the Rat River, Millen and three others fired a volley of bullets into the timber where Johnson was known to be hiding. They missed. Then Albert Johnson fired at Millen. Millen fell, dead almost instantly.

On the front page of the February 1, 1932, issue of the Toronto *Globe* was the following headline:

"RAT RIVER MADMAN KILLS POLICEMAN. HOLDS OFF OTHERS."

CHAPTER FIVE

Alone in the wilds I was happy,
In a cabin that I called my home,
Surrounded by mountains and valleys,
But the law wouldn't leave me alone.

In the latter part of July 1931, Albert Johnson left
Fort McPherson and paddled downstream in his large,
newly purchased canoe. It rode low in the water from
the weight of implements, supplies, and ammunition—not to mention two rifles, a shotgun, and a pair
of automatic pistols. Definitely, he expected trouble
of some kind.

Arthur Blake, a trader who had a store at the
mouth of the Husky River, told the police that early
in August 1931 a stranger he believed to have been
Albert Johnson had paddled a large canoe up a creek
behind the store. This creek led to the Rat River by a
chain of lake portages. Blake added that at the time
he did not think it possible for one man with so large
a canoe to reach the Rat River. In fact, Blake had
shouted out as much to the stranger. But the other
only shot him an angry glance and continued on.

And why not? As the vast Northland was soon to
learn, Albert Johnson was very adept at doing the
apparently impossible. He accomplished it with an
ease that made it seem routine.

A few weeks after leaving Fort McPherson, Albert Johnson was building a small cabin on the site he had selected. It was on a high bluff, surrounded by patches of brush, overlooking the swift-moving Rat River that rushed on to meet Driftwood Creek, fifteen miles away. And the manner in which he built his cabin proves that he was expecting trouble. So, in his methodical way, he prepared to meet it.

As an inspection later showed, the logs he used were a foot in diameter. The inside dimensions were roughly ten by fourteen feet. As for the unusually thick and heavy door, it stood four feet high, only three feet of which was above ground level. The roof was made of sturdy poles covered with frozen sod two feet in thickness. The walls were reinforced with extra logs and more frozen sod up to a height twenty inches above the ground. The floor of the structure was two feet below ground level, which provided protection in the event of a siege. And, for a final touch, the far-thinking Rat River Trapper cleverly fashioned out loopholes above the bottom logs in eight important locations around his fortress.

Finally, his cabin constructed and well provisioned, armed with his five guns and a large supply of ammunition, Albert Johnson was ready to take on all comers.

It was in the month of August that the cabin was completed. A month during which a certain beauty reigns, particularly in the southern areas of the Northwest Territories—as though the elements wish to compensate the inhabitants for the long months of snow behind them and those which will soon come again. So there is that brief period of comparative warmth, with the woodlands a blaze of brilliant colours.

The countless streams and lakes throughout the region contain salmon, rainbow trout, and lake trout, as well as other varieties of fish. The vast plains, woods, mountains, and valleys teem with game— black, brown, and grizzly bear, caribou, fox, wolverine, beaver, and Great Stone sheep. Moose crash through leafy forests and swim in the cold streams. Wolf packs are numerous, and from high plateaus mountain goats survey the world beneath them in dignified silence. Overhead wing myriad birds, including the large and majestic golden eagle. Horned owls hoot in the tree tops.

But summer is fleeting, and by mid September there are many signs of oncoming winter. Mosquitoes and black-flies disappear. The forests lose their brilliant colours and the winds become colder. Caribou instinctively sense what is to follow and start to gather for migration, while massive flocks of geese make ready for their long flight southward to the Gulf of Mexico.

In October 1931, somewhere not far from his cabin on the high bluff overlooking the Rat River, Albert Johnson came upon four Louchoux Indians, members of a party camped six miles upstream in some deserted cabins that had survived the gold-rush days. Rifle in hand, he angrily ordered them to be on their way and never to return to his territory. Those flashing green eyes had their usual effect on Indians, and they fled before him, muttering, "He has death in his eyes."

But an old saying tells us that there are exceptions to all rules. If we are to believe one story, his warning did not necessarily apply to all Indians. This story has it that, unseen in the dead of night, while stars glittered and the world slept, on several occasions an Indian maid went quite willingly—and even un-invited—to the cabin of Albert Johnson. She is said to have been an unusually comely daughter of the forest.

In late December 1931 began the series of events that started the Arctic Circle War.

Several Indians who had been trapping in the Rat River district came to the post of the R.C.M.P. at Arctic Red River and reported their grievances to Constable Millen. It was a dire tale they had to tell. According to them, they were being victimized as well as terrorized by a strange white man who lived in a cabin fifteen miles up the Rat River. Not only had he ordered them to leave the district, he had also found their traplines, flung the bait away, smashed their traps with heavy boulders, and then tied them to the limbs of trees. Why, he had even destroyed their rabbit snares. One of them said that he believed the name of the culprit was Albert Johnson.

Constable Millen was quick to remember. Albert Johnson? Why, of course. Only the previous summer, in Fort McPherson, he had talked with Albert Johnson. He also recalled telling the man that, if he intended to trap in the Rat River area, he must first get a trapper's licence. And to the best of Millen's knowledge there was no record of his having done so. Therefore, action must be taken.

At 7:00 in the morning on December 26, Mounties Alfred "Bunce" King and Joseph Bernard left Arctic Red River by dog-sled for the Rat River. It was bitterly cold, but the huskies, fresh and eager, flung themselves against their harness to plow steadily ahead, and snow clods flew from their paws. It could

have been that neither lawman was overly enthu-
siastic about the trip, as it represented a two-and-a-
half-day journey each way. And all for something
that was of little importance. Only a routine check.

The Mounties spent the first night of their journey
at Fort McPherson and the second in a hastily
constructed camp at the mouth of the Rat River. The
following morning, December 28, 1931, they left
early to cover the remaining fifteen miles to the
isolated cabin of Albert Johnson, and around 11:00 it
came into view.

Forty yards from the cabin, the Mounties brought
their dog-teams to a halt beside a heavy patch of
brush, and then turned to gaze at the weird structure
before them. There was something almost awesome
about the place; with its three-foot-high door and
bizarre construction, it could have passed as the
jumbled abode of some eccentric midget. A recent
fall of snow had obliterated any tracks and the area
around the cabin was an unbroken sweep of
whiteness. Over all was a complete silence. But the
sharp eyes of the men were quick to notice a curl of
smoke rising from the chimney.

Then, as the dogs began an impatient whining, the
nostrils of both men picked up the tantalizing odours
of brewing coffee and frying bacon. A glow of
anticipation lit their eyes. King turned to Bernard.

"Let's hope this Albert Johnson is a hospitable
gent and invites us in. A cup of hot coffee would hit
the spot."

With that, Mountie King, leaving his companion to
keep an eye on the dogs, walked briskly through the
unmarked snow to the cabin door. He raised a
mittened hand, gave two sharp raps on the door, and
called out:

"Mr. Johnson. Are you there, Mr. Johnson?"

The only answer was silence. In a report to his commanding officer, King later wrote: "I spent nearly a half-hour at the cabin of Albert Johnson, knocking on the door and calling out to Johnson. Several times I informed him who I was and that I wished to speak to him. Yet he refused to open the door or answer. He made no response of any kind. But he was there. Once I saw him peeping at me through a small window near the door, which he immediately covered when he saw me looking at him."

King finally returned to Bernard and the two dog-teams beside the brush. The Mounties held a brief conference and decided there was only one logical course to follow. Despite the cold, they would push on to Aklavik and obtain a search warrant, as there appeared to be no other way they could hope to question Albert Johnson. To be sure, Aklavik was eighty miles away. With the return trip it represented a hundred and sixty miles in all. And to travel such a distance across snow-covered wastes by dog-sled, with the thermometer hovering at fifty below, is no picnic.

Through his small window by the door, Albert Johnson, eyes narrowed, watched the officers take their departure. The route they were taking told him where they were going. And he realized why, and he knew they would soon return. Bringing others with them.

CHAPTER SIX

An Indian maid came to my cabin,
Breathless and wide-eyed with fear.
She warned that the Mounties were coming,
And said: "We better get out of here."

Anu, the Indian maid that legend links with Albert
Johnson, is said to have been born in Spatsizi, a
rugged area in a remote section of the vast Cassiar
District of northern British Columbia.

Spatsizi is today practically as little known to the
outside world as it was in the days of Stanley Black,
the first white man to enter the territory, in 1834. It
has an average elevation of 2,500 feet, with its highest
point—8,000 feet—at Cold Fish Lake. The waters of
the great Klappan and Stikine rivers surround the
3,600 square miles of mountain wilderness. A forgotten world, swarming with game and fish-choked
streams, its lush valleys have escaped the impact of
civilization.

The name Spatsizi is the Tahitan Indian word for
"red goat", for there the goats roll in the red
sandstone of the mountain slopes.

Anu was the daughter of a Tahitan woman and a
white man. One of the few white men who were even
aware of the existence of Spatsizi. The reason for his

going to that mountain wilderness is unknown. But he stayed there, and lived in affectionate happiness with his wife and family. Evidently a man of learning, he taught his children to read and write the language of the white man, and he brought them up in fear of the Lord.

The family lived near the small Indian settlement that was to be known later as Telegraph Creek. It was there, on numerous nights, as his wife looked placidly on, that the white father would tell the fascinated Anu, her older brother, and her little sister of the wonders of the outside world.

By the time she had reached the age of eighteen, it was evident that nature had been unusually generous to Anu. The blood of her father was apparent, her complexion being olive rather than the darker hue of the other maids of her tribe. Many admiring glances, some secretive, some downright open and frank, were cast her way by the men.

It was in that summer—1926—that the stranger came into her life. She and her mother were several miles from their native village, hunting for the ginseng roots the Tahitan tribe used for medicine, when they suddenly realized they had strayed between a she-grizzly and her cubs. They had stopped beside a tree to enjoy the snack they had brought with them, when the two frolicking cubs tumbled out of a near-by weed patch. The next moment, the she-bear—a half-ton of fury with shovel-size paws and foot-long claws—was charging.

Two rifle shots snapped out, the assault was checked, and the great bear crashed to the earth. As the startled gaze of Anu swept around her to find the source of that gunfire, a white man with a smoking gun emerged from the trees. A trail-pack was strapped to his shoulders. He wore heavy boots that went half way to his knees, laced with strips of rawhide. A black hat was pushed back on his head. His features were stern, his eyes were hard. It was Albert Johnson.

The mother of Anu, in her Tahitan tongue, broke into profuse thanks to the stranger for saving their lives. She hoped the Great Spirit would always watch over him and guide his moccasin steps. Also, that he would raise numerous children, have an obedient wife, grow fat, and know many years. She invited him to her dwelling with offers of every delicacy from caribou steaks to boiled beaver tails.

But when the stranger showed little interest at such fare and did not even condescend to answer, Anu thought to speak in the English her father had taught her.

"My mother thanks you for saving our lives and so do I. She would like you to come and meet my father so he may thank you. Can you understand me? Do you know what I am saying?"

He nodded.

"Then you will come with us and share our food?"

Albert Johnson shook his head and made as though to take his departure. But, as his gaze fell on the two cubs, a thought seemed to strike him. He swung his rifle onto his back, reached down for the cubs, and put one under each arm.

"They are too young to fend for themselves. I will follow the trail left by their mother and return them to where they belong."

That was all. The man walked away from them with no further words and soon disappeared among the trees.

Five years were to pass before she saw him again.

On this day in late October 1931, Anu made her way along the desolate shore of the narrow Rat River. The lush valleys of her mountain homeland, Spatsizi, were now six hundred miles to the south. There had been many changes in the life of Anu since the day the stern and silent stranger shot down the grizzly and saved her life. But she had never forgotten the man. Even when she eventually learned from her tribesmen that he had left Spatsizi for the world far to the north, she continued to hope he might some day return. She often wondered what his name was and where he came from. And if there might be moments in his lonely life when he sometimes thought of her.

The inhabitants of Spatsizi rarely left their peaceful world, since for them it had everything they needed, in abundant quantities. But there had been a few who did forsake the land of their ancestors, and among these was the sister of Anu's mother. The aunt and her husband had heard tales of the wonderful things that could be had in the outside world if you could get a strange commodity that the white man called "money".

The couple had been told that to secure this mysterious "money", which endowed its owner with great powers, was comparatively simple. All one had to do was to take the skins of various animals to certain white men who were known as "traders". They in turn would give you the money that supplied all wants and wishes. It was as easy as that. So the aunt and her husband, who were both experienced trappers, had waved good-bye to friends and relatives.

They went to Aklavik, six hundred miles to the north, and never returned.

Eventually, the white father of Anu realized over the years that there was one mistake he had made. When he had told his children of the lands beyond their mountains, he had made his stories too interesting. This was apparent when, one day in the late spring of 1928, Anu's brother, twenty-two years old and a husky six-footer, announced to his father that he and his sister planned to leave Spatsizi and see the lands beyond its borders. Anu was twenty at the time.

The surprised father described their plans to his Indian wife, who in turn drew Anu aside to ask: "Is it true that you and your brother are leaving your homeland?"

"Yes, mother. It is true."

"I understand your brother's reason for wishing to travel far. Like most young men, he wants to see what is beyond the next hill. But your purpose, Anu, brings disgrace on my head as well as your own, for I know what it is. You hope to find the strange white man you so often talk about. The one you saw two years ago for the length of thirty heartbeats. A man whose name you do not even know. You plan to search the world till you find him and then give yourself to him."

"What can I hope to find here?" was Anu's response.

"Your choice of any young man in our land. They all want you and you know it. Here, you may have all you could ever hope for. A man who will work, hunt, and provide for you. You can live with honour, have children who obey and respect you, as well as know that the Gods of your ancestors smile down upon you. For you will be living the good life that pleases them."

"Suppose I choose to live a life that pleases myself?"

"Anu, how can you think like that? Even if you did find the stranger and went to his sleeping blankets, once he tired of you he would throw you out of his dwelling. White men soon tire of Indian women, even one as pretty as yourself. They usually leave them or kill them."

"But you are Indian and father is a white man. Did he ever tire of having you, or throw you out of his dwelling? Did he ever leave you or try to kill you?"

The mother sighed and raised a hand to her brow. When she spoke again, her voice was quiet and resigned.

"Very well, Anu. I will not try to stop you. But remember, even if you do find him, the day will come when you will wish you had not. That instead of saving you, it would have been far better if he had held his fire and let the bear destroy you. At least, that way, death would have been fast, the suffering soon over."

With that grim warning, her mother turned away, and it was apparent she wished to say no more about the matter. Perhaps she realized that further words would be useless. Later the father tried to dissuade his two eldest offspring. But, youth being not easily discouraged, a few weeks later Anu and her stalwart brother, packs strapped to their shoulders, took their departure from their homeland. For days the two marched steadily northward. Always on and on, across a seemingly endless world of rivers, streams, plains, and forests that stretched away to the sky. For Anu's ultimate goal, like that of her aunt ten years earlier, was Aklavik. She had been told it was the home of many white men.

The rifle of Anu's brother supplied them with game, the numerous lakes and streams provided fish. Again it was the month of June, the beginning of the Northland's brief summer, and both the deep snows and appalling cold had temporarily vanished. Each dusk the two would quickly erect a small lean-to. With the dawn they would be once more on their way. They passed through many districts, they saw numerous strange faces, but all in all what they experienced was not greatly different from the life they had known.

They found, as it always is in the wilds, that life is a battle for survival.

However, neither Anu nor her brother had been without finances when they left Spatsizi: its abundant wildlife made it a veritable paradise for the hunter. The brother carried a number of fine skins that could bring good prices in the outside world. As for Anu, the departing gift of her father, along with some golden advice, had been a collector's dream of pelts—a number of valuable silver fox skins. Moreover, along their route to Aklavik, both brother and sister showed a canny knowledge of the value of their furs and a surprising gift of salesmanship as they bartered in the stores of various traders.

Finally, upon reaching Aklavik, they sold their remaining hides and promptly made for the bank where each opened an account—a negotiation that showed they had not forgotten the teachings of their father. Then they found the home of their aunt and uncle.

During the following two years, while her brother and uncle went out on their traplines, Anu assisted her now ailing aunt with the household duties and kept a sharp lookout for the stranger she had journeyed so far to find. The presence of the comely young Tahitan was soon noticed by the local gentry, merchants, trappers, and prospectors and a number of them approached Anu with offers. But she refused. There could be but one man in her life.

In the spring of 1931, Anu's brother returned to Aklavik from his traplines with a wife, a plump and mannish-featured woman of the Louchoux tribe. With the coming of fall, the two made ready to return to her tribesmen for a season of trapping in the Rat River district, eighty miles to the south. Anu's brother asked her to go with them. His wife was soon expecting their first child, and Anu's help would be invaluable during the long winter months to come. Then, with the return of spring, she could come back to Aklavik and continue her search for the stranger. Anu agreed.

So it came about that on a day in late October 1931, the twenty-three-year-old Anu made her way along the shore of the Rat River. Five miles behind her was the encampment of twenty or so Louchoux Indians, most of whom were out on their traplines. With them was Anu's brother, whose pregnant wife awaited his return in one of several cabins that had been built in bygone days.

Anu had wandered far that day. She had left her brother's wife secure in the cabin and gone forth with no set destination. She wished only to be alone with her thoughts. Almost unmindful of her surroundings, eventually she reached and climbed a high bluff overlooking the river a hundred feet below her. She knew that sensation of superiority one inevitably experiences when gazing at the world from a commanding height. But then her eyes swept to the east. A gasp escaped her lips.

Less than two hundred yards away was the outline of a small cabin. One of such strange construction it appeared the creation of a nightmare. And she realized where her heedless footsteps had been taking her—she had somehow stumbled upon the abode of the terrible man so feared by the Louchoux Indians.

For days she had heard them speak of little else, as they told how he had cruelly destroyed the traps that represented their sole source of income. Only a week before, four of them had gone to him to demand that he stop interfering with their traplines. But while still some distance from his cabin he had met them, rifle in hand and a gleam in his eye that caused them to turn and flee. The four were as one in agreeing that he was not human but an evil being of some kind beyond their experience. They reported that he had shouted after them, that if they ever returned he would kill them all.

Anu caught her breath and wheeled, preparing to run as she had never run before. But too late. At the same instant, like the angry report of a rifle, one word snapped out:

"Stop!"

Heart pounding, she froze in terrified rigidity for several seconds before she ventured a sideways glance. At first she saw only a man who wore a parka and a black fur hat, striding rapidly towards her. Then she saw his swarthy features, his menacing scowl, his narrowed eyes, and his rifle.

But Anu did not quail before him. Instead she needed only that one glance for a wild joy to surge through her being. She knew her years of searching were over.

Her dark eyes were wide, her features lit with a smile of realization. Her hand was extended as the man came to a sharp halt scarcely three paces from her.

"It is you," were Anu's first words. "It really is. At last I have found you."

The other made no reply, though his silent glare did not abate. But this did not discourage Anu.

"Don't you remember me? Five years ago in far-off Spatsizi, our beautiful land to the south, you saved my mother and me from a she-grizzly who thought we were going to harm her cubs. Later we both asked you to come to our dwelling, but you refused. Instead, you picked up the two cubs, said you would return them to a place of safety, and then went on your way. My heart was sad.

"So I never did get to see you again," she added, "though I later learned you had left Spatsizi and gone northward. Finally I could stand it no longer. I left my people and journeyed north. I have spent lonely years in searching for you. Finally the spirits of my ancestors, knowing my sadness, have guided my moccasins this way. I want to thank you. I want to be with you."

"You wait five years then journey six hundred miles to thank me for shooting a bear? Bah! It is an Indian trick—the kind a squaw who hungers to share the blankets of a white man would use."

"But it is no trick," cut in Anu, "and I have never shared the blankets of any man in my life. I only wanted to see you. To talk with you. Please hear me."

She told him there was no deceit or treachery in her heart. That she wished only to serve and would follow him to the ends of the earth. She could provide the food for them both, she would ask for nothing, and there was no mountain too high for her to climb if he wished it. It was he alone, his safety, comfort, and health, that mattered to her.

Anu went on to explain that she did not expect an immediate answer. He should have time to carefully consider the proposition that she become his woman. It would be best for both of them, as one should not be hasty when confronted by such decisions. Then, when the allotted time had passed, she would return for his answer. One that she felt confident would be in the affirmative, since, as she pointed out:

"Surely the Gods, in their wisdom, would not have willed that we meet again, unless some unusual future awaits us. It may be one of continued peace and joy. It could be one of death and violence, with many enemies howling for our blood. But be assured, whatever it is I will remain at your side and not falter. My father taught me well how to handle a gun."

The steely eyes of Albert Johnson had never left hers, though his set features gave no indication of having heard a word she said.

"I will be going, now," Anu concluded in her soft voice. "I shall return to the encampment of the Louchoux tribe, six miles upstream, where I am staying in a cabin. If you wish to see me before the allotted time, it will be a simple matter to do so. If not, I will wait till three moons have passed and then return here."

With that she took her departure.

CHAPTER SEVEN

I saw Mountie King approach my cabin.
So I reached for my rifle and said
"Cops that call on the Rat River Trapper,
Can expect to be met with hot lead."

On December 29, 1931, Constables King and Bernard of the R.C.M.P. arrived in Aklavik, half-frozen, their dog-teams exhausted, after completing the eighty-mile trip from the cabin of the Rat River Trapper. As Aklavik was the Western Arctic Sub-District of the R.C.M.P., they went directly to headquarters and reported to Inspector A. N. Eames.

Alexander Neville Eames is a name that will long be remembered in the Northland. He was a man with sterling qualities, scrupulously fair in his judgment of others. Eames had joined the force back in 1913. During thirty-three years' service, he eventually rose to the position of Assistant Commander before his retirement in 1946.

Inspector Eames viewed with some concern the report of King and Bernard on the strange behaviour of the Rat River Trapper in his lonely and oddly built cabin. They said that without doubt the man must have heard the many loud knocks on his door, as well as King's shouts requesting permission to speak to him. Also, King had certainly had a glimpse of Albert Johnson peeking at him from the small window near the door. Undoubtedly an odd way to act for a man who had nothing to fear from the law.

After some thought, Inspector Eames issued a search warrant, and in view of Johnson's unusual attitude he decided that the two constables should take reinforcements with them on their return journey to the cabin. Sharp at 7:00 on the following morning, while it was still dark, King and Bernard, with fresh dogs, began their eighty-mile mush back to the cabin, accompanied by Constables Robert McDowell and Lazarus Sittichiulis.

The dog-teams went steadily ahead, and the shouts of their drivers rang out in the surrounding stillness as they passed across the snow-covered tundra. They made a hasty camp at nightfall, and the following morning at 10:30—the last day of the old year—once again the ugly cabin of Albert Johnson hove into view.

Although they had no way of knowing it, within that small structure a pair of agate-hard eyes were watching their every movement.

Again King and Bernard brought their dog-teams to a halt beside the heavy patch of brush forty yards from the cabin. The eerie silence of their first visit still prevailed, and King noticed that another snowfall had obliterated all tracks. He glanced up to the chimney.

"See that smoke? It tells that he's in there, just like he was the last time. Only now I have a search warrant and he'll either open the door or I'll break it in. He can have his choice. Wait here. It won't take me long."

"Watch yourself," advised Bernard.

The others could hear the crunch of his footsteps through the unmarked snow as he made his way to the cabin. One of the huskies started howling as he paused before the door. Once more King raised a mittened hand, knocked twice sharply, and called out:

"Mr. Johnson. Are you there, Mr. Johnson?"

Albert Johnson left no doubt as to his being there. His answer came almost immediately. Constable King was spun half around by the force of the rifle bullet before he plunged headlong into the snow.

The cruel and unexpected shooting of their fellow officer instantly removed all hopes of the Mounties for a peaceful settlement with Albert Johnson.

King had scarcely struck the snow before the three constables at the brush patch opened up with a barrage upon the cabin, forty yards away. Crouched low over their guns as they fired, the men advanced in a half-running zig-zag, to lessen the chances of the man in the cabin scoring another hit.

Albert Johnson fired again, and a bullet buzzed a scant half-inch past Mountie McDowell's face.

It was not till then that the three men realized the magnitude of the danger they were up against—that a lot of them might well be shot down and their frozen bodies left for the first passing wolf pack. For they suddenly became aware of the loopholes just above the bottom logs of the cabin. There were eight of them around the four walls: built-in firing stations. They realized why the floor of the cabin was below ground level, why the walls were reinforced by extra logs and frozen sod. The cabin was a veritable fortress. Johnson, in warmth and comfort, could take his time and pick them off one by one.

Then McDowell noticed a movement from the prostrate Mountie in the snow. Constable King was not dead. Seriously wounded to be sure, but still alive. While the rifles of his fellow officers fired steadily, King struggled to his feet, dazed, blood crimsoning the snow beneath him.

McDowell, having just reloaded, paused to empty the contents of his rifle at the loopholes in Albert Johnson's cabin, then ran forward to assist the swaying King. With the arm of the wounded man around his shoulder, McDowell started towards the brush patch and the dog-teams. Bernard and Sittichiulis sent bullet after bullet towards the loopholes in an attempt to draw off Johnson's fire as the two men plodded with agonizing slowness towards safety.

Finally having reached the brush, McDowell got his helpless burden onto a dog-sled and made him as comfortable as possible in the bitter cold and the icy winds. He then reloaded his empty rifle and, stepping from the brush and risking any gunfire that might come from the cabin, called out to the two constables to join him, while he sent a deluge of lead towards the small fortress to cover their retreat.

Crouched low and withdrawing slowly, but keeping up a steady fusillade as they did so, Sittichiulis and Bernard soon reached McDowell in the seclusion of the brush patch. The huskies in their harness were whining nervously. King had lapsed into unconsciousness. His stillness roused one of the men to shout back to the rifleman in the cabin:

"You murdering bastard!"

Immediately another shot answered him. But the brush screened them adequately. The bullet buzzed harmlessly by and continued on.

The three Mounties faced a grave situation. Constable King, seriously if not mortally wounded, must have medical attention as soon as possible. Every moment in that world of snow and cold lessened his chances.

"Let's face it," McDowell said, "as things stand now we haven't a chance against that fellow. The only way to get him out of there is with dynamite. Yes, that's the ticket! Dynamite. Ding him and his cabin to hell. Sure, we can return with explosives."

His listeners agreed. "Right. Thirty or more pounds, with caps and fuse, then come back here, and Johnson will find that it's not like shooting fish in a barrel. Next time it will be a different story."

McDowell put in: "Meanwhile, how about King? Are we just going to stand here?"

There could be but one logical answer. Though it must have galled them, circumstances compelled them to retreat. The dog-teams were wheeled around and the men mushed on, with the same thoughts predominant in the minds of each. Retaliation would come.

But first they must get King to the All Saints Mission in Aklavik, into the skilled care of Surgeon J. A. Urquhart.

From the small window near his cabin door, Albert Johnson saw the Royal Canadian Mounted Police retreat before him for the second time.

CHAPTER EIGHT

Once again Mounties came to my cabin.
There were nine men in all, it is true.
So with rifle in hand, I called to them:
"Come on, gents, I've been waiting for you."

From a career of more than twenty-eight years as an officer of the R.C.M.P., Robert G. McDowell's most vivid memory was of his wild dash across the dreary wastes to Aklavik, driving the dog-sled that carried the wounded Constable King. With Mounties Bernard and Sittichiulis driving the other teams, the distance was covered in the record time of eighteen hours.

A harsh ordeal under adverse conditions, it was primary in saving the life of Constable King. He not only recovered from his wound but served twenty-two more years on the force before he retired in 1953. In later life he was to be pointed out as "the first Mountie to be shot by the Rat River Trapper". King was also the only Mountie to survive one of Albert Johnson's bullets.

Immediately upon arriving in Aklavik, after taking King to the Mission, McDowell, Sittichiulis, and Bernard went directly to police headquarters. Eyes opened wide when they made their reports. Shocked by the shooting of King, Inspector Eames was also surprised to learn of the fortified construction of the cabin. Proof that, at the time he erected his cabin, Albert Johnson was expecting violent days ahead.

Buy why? That was the big question. Why? What reason could a man have for wanting to go out into a desolate wilderness, provide himself with provisions, guns, and ammunition, and put up an armed defence in an almost impenetrable fortress? It seemed incredible.

Thus, in view of all the mystery, as well as the seriousness of the criminal charges now facing Albert Johnson, Inspector Eames decided to lead a large party in person to that strange and lonely cabin near the Rat River. It would be a hand-picked posse of experienced officers and guides, seasoned to the rigours of the Arctic. They would be well supplied with provisions and ammunition in the event of a siege, with each man aware of the dangers. As an added precaution, Eames decided to bring along twenty pounds of dynamite.

Rumours naturally began to spread through Aklavik. Constable King had been shot by "a crazy trapper named Johnson who lives in the Rat River district". But as often happens, practically every time the tale was told it was given a new twist, till finally the gunman was regarded as a fiend incarnate. Then other tales were heard.

Hunters and trappers, brows wrinkled in thought as they smoked their pipes, began to recall certain incidents. Several of them mentioned having met a man named Johnson, far out in vast wilderness areas of both the Northwest Territories and the Yukon. They all agreed that the man was a "surly, sullen brute who carried a trail-pack and rifle, rarely spoke, and had green eyes".

Someone remembered a few years back, up in the northern Baker Lake district, having spoken to an Eskimo of the Netsilik tribe. The Eskimo had spoken of a strange white man known as Johnson, who once passed through the territory, whom his tribesmen had called "the man who steals gold from men's teeth".

A trapper named Daws had a story to tell of a recent experience with Albert Johnson. Only three months earlier, when in the Rat River district, Daws was passing the man's cabin and decided to drop in for a chat and a meal. Trappers are usually generous to those of their own ilk, as their presence is a welcome respite from months of loneliness. But Albert Johnson had shouted at Daws to be off, said if he came that way again he would kill him, then slammed the door in his face.

But, of all the stories told of a personal experience with Albert Johnson, the one related by a trapper named Bradley was the most intriguing, and was later at least partly authenticated.

On a fall day in 1931 a trapper paddled a canoe up to the wharf of the trading store of Arthur Blake at the mouth of the Husky River. As well as Blake, there were three other men in the store at the time of his arrival. He was barely through the doorway before he started talking:

"Boys, my name is Steve Bradley, I get around quite a bit and my headquarters are where I set down my hindquarters, but there is one thing I would like to know. What in hell is the matter with that fellow Albert Johnson who lives up the Rat on the north side? Just yesterday I was paddling along and saw him on the shore, and I've known him for several years, so

I called out to him and started to work my canoe to the shore for a pow-wow, when what do you think?"

"What?" asked one of the men.

"Why he was going to kill me, that's what," was the prompt reply of Bradley. "He whipped out a long hunting-knife from his belt. Shouted for me to get going or he would cut out my heart and feed it to the wolves. I got cracking. Fast."

There was a surprised silence while the men exchanged glances, and smoke-rings from pipes rose lazily to the ceiling. Then one of the listeners replied:

"Johnson has only been around here for a short while, but already the Indians are telling strange stories about him. They say he has gone brush-crazy."

Trader Blake asked Bradley: "But you said you've known Johnson for several years. Where did you first meet him and how?"

"At Fort Reliance in the spring of 1930. I had just been seven months around Breed's Lake, and had come to Reliance to sell my pelts, take it easy for a few weeks, and mingle with folks. I had only been there a couple of days when Albert Johnson drifted in. He looked the same then as he does now. Grim. I never knew him to smile. Folks shied away from him. They feared him and he knew it."

Johnson had rented a shack near Fort Reliance. The owner had told Bradley that the man spent most of his time in lying on his bunk and staring at the ceiling.

"Then one day two olds friends of mine, trappers named Bode and Olsen, came to Fort Reliance. I had known them for years. We used to call them the 'Gold-dust Twins' because both of them had pieces of gold in their teeth. They stayed around for several days and we had a high old time. Then they bought their provisions and said they were off to the Granite Falls district. That I wouldn't be seeing them for quite a while."

Several months passed. Bradley was now living in a cabin some miles south of the Thalon River, where he had set out traplines and was preparing to spend the winter. Then, one fall night, he answered an unexpected knock on his door to once more stare into the hard eyes of Albert Johnson. Surprised, he had invited the other to supper and a night's lodging.

But Albert Johnson only shook his head impatiently.

"I don't want your food, shelter, or company. I am here only for information. Do I make myself clear?"

Bradley nodded.

"Those two friends of yours I used to see you with last spring when you were in Fort Reliance. The name of one of them is Bode?"

"Of course," was Bradley's answer. "You mean Emil Bode and Jan Olsen. Old friends of mine."

"Right," replied Albert Johnson. "They're the two I want. I have important business with them. Unfinished business that I must take care of at once. Where can I find them?"

"Find them? Why they'll be at their camp near Granite Falls. That's about sixty-five miles from here, and to get there you go north-east for——."

"I'll find them."

With that, Albert Johnson turned and walked rapidly away into the cold and blackness of the Arctic night.

"That was a year ago, and the last time I saw Albert Johnson till yesterday," Bradley was presently informing his four listeners.

"As I say," he went on, "when I saw Johnson on the Rat River, he whipped out a hunting knife and told me to get going. So I went, but then he yelled out that he'd found those friends of mine and finished his business with them.

"Now I wonder what sort of business he would have been talking about?"

Early in January of 1932, near the Thalon River in the Northwest Territories, a trapper named Croft made a gruesome discovery. What he found was reported on the front page of the January 5, 1932, issue of the Toronto *Globe.*

TWO TRAPPERS DEAD, MURDER SUSPECTED
Year Old Tragedy of Barren Lands
Investigated by Mounted Police

"Fort Resolution, N.W.T., Jan. 4: Jan Olsen and Emil Bode, two well known Barren Land trappers, were found dead at their camp on the Thalon River in the vicinity of Granite Falls, about 150 miles east of Fort Reliance. They were found by Clark Croft, another Barren Land trapper, who sent word out by Indians to the Royal Canadian Mounted Police detachment at Fort Reliance.

"Olsen and Bode left Reliance during March, 1930, for their trapping grounds, taking with them two years supply of food and clothing. Cause of death is unknown, but it could not be starvation, for plenty of food and clothing were found in their cache, just a short distance from their tent in which they were found dead. It is stated they must have died about a year ago. According to Indians who brought out the news, they thought there had been foul play."

From Aklavik, on January 3, 1932, Inspector A. N. Eames and seven followers began their journey by dog-sled to the lonely cabin of Albert Johnson.

The men that accompanied the Inspector were all experienced manhunters: Mounties McDowell, Sittichiulis, Bernard, and Millen, as well as trappers Karl Gardlund, Knud Lang, and Ernest Sutherland. There were forty-two dogs to pull the sleds and twenty pounds of dynamite, to be used to blast the walls of the cabin if the Rat River Trapper refused to surrender.

The eight-man posse reached the mouth of the Rat River on January 5. The stock of dog food was replenished at Arthur Blake's nearby trading store on the Husky River. Here they were joined by the experienced Indian guide, Charlie Rat, who arrived from Fort McPherson where he had been celebrating the New Year. It was Charlie Rat's mission to guide the party along an Indian trapline south of the Rat River.

Inspector Eames had decided, and wisely, that for the posse to travel along the river itself would be to court disaster. The river granted a crack shot like Albert Johnson too many opportunities for ambush.

For it is as though nature provided the lower reaches of the Rat River for the express purpose of a surprise attack on an invading force. It is there that the water runs through the gigantic canyon which in some places is as much as twelve hundred yards wide. The awesome banks lining the river frequently tower to a height of seven hundred feet. Again, the valley itself is well timbered and covered with brush.

Several unforeseen misfortunes struck at the posse soon after leaving Blake's Trading Store. First, the bitter cold increased till the thermometer finally dropped to fifty-five below. Then the usually dependable Charlie Rat erred badly in his judgment. The first night, when the posse went into camp, the Indian assured Inspector Eames that they were only four miles below Johnson's cabin. The next day it was eventually learned that they were instead six miles above it. This made it necessary to spend the remainder of day, January 8, in returning to the camp of the previous night.

The following day, with the intense cold snapping at the breath, travel was tortuous. The dangerous footing through the loose snow and willows resulted in a number of painful falls that further slowed progress. Consequently, that night they were still some miles from their objective. It was a discouraged as well as exhausted party that finally made camp.

That night, a check revealed that there was less than two days' supply of food left for the dogs. With conditions going from bad to worse and nothing that promised a change for the better, immediate action was imperative. Inspector Eames announced that, shortly after the coming dawn, they would reach and storm the stronghold.

Around noon on the following day, which would be about an hour after daybreak at that time of year in the Arctic, the nine weary men came within half a mile of the cabin, and halted.

Last-minute advice was given as the dogs were being secured to some timber not far from the river bank. Of course there was no knowing when murderous rifle fire might come from the loopholes, but cautiously the men, watchful, rifles before them, edged forward through the mist of swirling snow, and partially surrounded the cabin.

Several of the men later reported that they could hear a din inside, "as though he was throwing frying pans around—then he started talking to himself."

Finally, after seeing that his men were in advantageous positions and nothing could be gained in further delay, Inspector Eames raised one hand to his mouth and shouted out:

"Albert Johnson, this is Inspector Eames of the Royal Canadian Mounted Police speaking. You are under arrest, and in the name of the law I demand that you come forward and keep your hands above your head."

CHAPTER NINE

I have never fled from beast or mortal.
I remain where I am, with my gun.
And when trouble comes, I'm there to meet it,
For I never learned how to run.

Constable King had been shot shortly before 11:00
a.m. on December 31, 1931. The following day,
Albert Johnson walked six miles up the shore of the
Rat River in the hope of finding the solution to a
problem—the welfare of the month-old puppy snugly
cuddled in his arms.

Of course, he had no way of knowing that Constable King would recover from his wound. Certain of
the officer's death, Albert Johnson regarded the
matter as closed. Proof that he wanted to be left
alone and was a dangerous man to visit.

At the same time he was well aware of the dire and
prompt punishment that would be meted out to the
killer of a member of the R.C.M.P. The Mounties, he
knew, would follow him to the ends of the earth if
need be. There was nowhere they could not search,
no place they would not go. More than that, they
would keep coming and coming, year after year. Yes,
and even if he shot them down again and again, there
would always be others coming after them.

However, there was no sign of fear in his face as he made his way up the north shore of the Rat River on that New Year's Day in 1932. It was also evident that he expected no immediate danger, as it was one of the very few times he failed to carry his rifle. His only weapon was a hunting knife in the leather sheath that hung from his belt. He wore a black fur hat and heavy fur-lined parka. Thick socks and long Eskimo boots known as "kamiks" protected his feet from the snow. His folded arms sheltered the puppy he carried.

He completed his six-mile walk at a small encampment of twenty Louchoux Indians who were trapping in that area.

Most of the men were out on their traplines and the camp was deserted, except for some of the women and a few dogs that barked at his approach. Just before him was the cabin, he had been told, where dwelt the one he had come to find. But before he reached the door, it was pulled back and she was framed in the opening.

Anu's first words were: "You have finally come and I am ready to go with you. Anywhere."

Some fifteen minutes later, it was a bewildered Anu who stood before the fireplace of the small cabin she shared with her brother and his wife.

Albert Johnson sat near by, the small pup at his feet.

"But I cannot understand you," Anu was saying. "Of course the news of your shooting the policeman reached us here, and my brother said he heard the sounds of distant gunfire when he was out on his traplines. He also told us what you yourself must know—that the scarlet-coats will return, and when they do they will hang you.

"Your only hope is for both of us to flee to some faraway place where no one will ever find us," she pointed out," and I thought that was why you came here. But now you say you do not intend to run away. That instead, you will go back to your cabin and fight it out with the Mounties when they return. You say you only want me to look after your little dog, so that he will not be in danger during the battle to come. Is that right?"

Albert Johnson nodded.

"But returning to your cabin is sheer madness! It is the first place the police will look for you. Can you not realize that?"

He made no reply, but his silence did not discourage her. For Anu had an idea how he might easily get away from the law.

"Now hear me," she insisted. "Listen and I will tell how you can escape from the police, and will never need to worry about them again."

The way she told it, it did seem to have possibilities. They must make ready for immediate flight to the south. But there would be a matter of disguise. He could wear her brother's garments. If he kept his hat pulled low, he could look like an Indian. As for herself, she would darken her light olive complexion that betrayed the blood of her white father. Then they would set forth through the snow.

After all, the police would be looking for a white man. The questions they would ask the inhabitants, in wilderness settlements and lonely outposts for hundreds of miles around, would all be about a solitary white man. A loner. No one would think to mention that an Indian and a dusky woman had passed their way.

As for themselves, she pointed out, they would be very careful to act in the manner expected of them and avoid speech with strangers. But all the while they would be making long marches southward, ever southward. They could conceal the footprints that could tell of their whereabouts by following in the tracks of wandering caribou.

"In time we will reach Spatsizi, my homeland. I can lead the way, for I have travelled it. Once there we will be safe and know the warmth and comforts of the dwelling of my parents, who will greet us with joy in their hearts. And if, on some distant day, the police should ever come, I can take you to forests so deep that they have yet to know the foot of man. Or else to mountain tops so high that only the eagles go there."

But a headshake was his only reply.

Nothing could sway Albert Johnson from his purpose to fight it out to the death with the Mounties. Almost angrily, Anu cried out:

"It is only for the sake of your foolish pride that you go back to your cabin. If you flee, you think the police will regard you as a coward!"

Albert Johnson nodded and said:

"I respect the wisdom of your advice, but I have never learned how to run."

With that, the Rat River Trapper stepped to the door and opened it. Dusk was falling and soon would come the pitch blackness of an Arctic night. Near by, several fires were glowing in the cabins of the Indian encampment. Before he left he turned once more to Anu:

"Thank you for your promise to look after the pup. I named him Ace."

Then he was gone.

CHAPTER TEN

For fifteen long hours the siege raged on,
Till at last the Mounties found that they
Were no match for the Rat River Trapper,
So they turned and they went on their way.

"BOMBS, RIFLES AND POSSE FAIL TO DIS-
LODGE TRAPPER FROM HIS CABIN-FORTRESS.
Mounted Police Withdraw To Replenish Food
Supplies, After Trapper Wins First Round of Siege.
Automatic In Each Hand, He Foils Repeated
Onslaughts."

The above appeared in headlines on page one in
that January 14, 1932, issue of the Toronto *Globe*.

The lengthy write-up that followed told in detail
of the grim battle that transpired when Inspector
Eames, along with his four Mounties and four trappers, sought to capture Albert Johnson in his isolated
stronghold.

The siege began around noon on January 10,
1932.

According to the accounts told of him, the Rat
River Trapper was in fine fettle that day. And he had
some new tricks prepared for the opposition. Anti-
cipating that they would use dynamite, he had dug a
deep tunnel beneath the dirt floor of the cabin—
rather like an air-raid shelter.

With the arrival of the police, proceedings got off to a slam-bang start. The shouted words of Inspector Eames had scarcely been uttered when the door of the cabin was kicked back and the Rat River Trapper stood in the opening. But his hands were not above his head. Instead they were extended before him, and in each was an automatic revolver which he immediately began to fire.

But, even as the first shots rang out, the posse members sought to make themselves difficult targets. Five of them hit the snow face down, practically burying themselves. The other four turned and scrambled over the bank of the bluff that led down to the frozen Rat River.

Those five who were buried in the snow now had to burrow their way like giant worms towards the others, who were in comparative safety behind the top of the bluff and who, with only their heads protruding above it, could send a deluge of lead towards the cabin to hold the fire of the Rat River Trapper until their comrades had moved.

Finally the five reached safety. Several shots came from the cabin as they flung themselves over the bank. But there were no casualties, and while three of the posse remained at the bank to exchange shots with Johnson, the others returned to the river's shore and started a roaring fire.

The remainder of that brief Arctic day was spent in taking potshots at the cabin. Its occupant returned the fire, bullet for bullet, but by some miracle the members of the posse were still unharmed.

In the fading rays of daylight, the sticks of dynamite, which had frozen, were slowly thawed out and made ready. From a protected place at the top of the bluff, several charges were flung towards the cabin. But as far as could be seen they did not have the slightest effect on the stronghold. In fact, some of them did not even so much as explode. Matters were rapidly becoming grim.

Then, as though these frustrations were not enough for the harassed Mounties, as daylight drifted into dark—around 4:00 p.m.—a series of dismal howls came from the woods near the river, and the remaining feed had to be divided among the forty-two huskies. Just where their next meal would come from was another problem.

After nightfall, the men decided to storm the cabin. It was a dark night and they were now almost invisible to the besieged marksman. All of them topped the bluff and began a stealthy advance towards the cabin, intending to break down the door and crash in.

Then they heard it. Loud and murderous blasts from the shack before them that the gun-wise men instantly recognized. Johnson was using a shotgun.

It was but another surprise that he had in readiness for that half-frozen and unfortunate party of man-hunters. Realizing that he would not be left in peace during the hours of darkness, Albert Johnson was now using a weapon whose spreading pellets made it dangerous in the extreme, regardless of the poor visibility. The odds against a miss were excellent. Again the shotgun roared out and lead flew in all directions.

But one of the posse threw a stick of dynamite that landed directly at the foot of the cabin door. And this one did explode. In the glow from the fireplace within, they could see the stout door tremble and swing back on damaged hinges. The next moment, however, two more shots came through the open doorway telling them that the cabin's occupant was still alive and full of fight.

Still, the posse raced forward and around the cabin, pouring bullets into the loopholes as well as through the window and open doorway. The reply was a rapid barrage from automatic revolvers. Albert Johnson, using every weapon in his arsenal, more than matched the fire of his attackers.

Sensing that reckless displays of bravery would soon result in death for his men, in view of the Rat River Trapper's seemingly endless supply of ammunition, Inspector Eames finally called to the others to join him at the edge of the bluff. As they did, trapper Knud Lang came forward excitedly.

"I saw him, Inspector. I had a good look at Albert Johnson. As I ran around the shack I got a bit of a look through the window and there he was."

"Go on," said Eames.

"I could see him in the light from the fireplace. He was on his knees. Three guns—two rifles and a shotgun—on the floor in front of him, and he had a pair of automatic pistols in his hands. Not only that, right behind him was the entrance to a tunnel he has dug out for himself. Looks like he's going to fight to the death."

Three other members of the posse had also had glimpses of Johnson and the tunnel. One of them, who had been at the rear of the shack looking through a loophole, said:

"He heard me. Oh, you can be sure of that, for he swung around and fired a revolver shot through the hole just as I pulled my head away. I could feel the bullet zinging past me."

More futile bullets were sent against the cabin. The night, if that were possible, grew colder. Then, around 3:00 a.m., Inspector Eames made one final effort. He gave the last of the dynamite to one of his men, with the instructions to go quietly forward and throw it onto the roof.

Eames produced two flashlights and handed one to trapper Karl Gardlund. "When the dynamite explodes on the roof, I am hoping it will blast a hole and at least stun Johnson. So when the charge goes off, you and I will race in the front door and shoot our spotlights into his face, temporarily blinding him. Then we can rush him, pounce on him, and overpower him. I want to take the man alive if possible. You understand?"

Gardlund nodded and the inspector turned to the others:

"Stay here. Your lives have already been endangered far too much. So stay here, and if Gardlund and I are lucky, we will call out to you."

So the three men crept forward on their missions, while behind them the others looked on, scarcely breathing, expecting a volley of bullets to come from the cabin at any moment. But no sound came from the cabin. The advance of the trio had apparently gone undetected. Was it possible that Albert Johnson, weary after many hectic hours, had dozed off?

A long ten minutes of silence.

Then a thunderous roar and flames flying skyward announced the success of the Mountie with the dynamite. His aim had been perfect. Heavy strips of wood and frozen sod shot up as a gaping hole was blasted in the cabin roof. The watching posse cheered.

Inspector Eames and Gardlund charged forward to take advantage of the havoc. They ran directly towards the door, switching on their flashlights. But Albert Johnson had not been stunned by the blast or even as much as shaken. That he was clear-headed was instantly proved by the accuracy of two bullets he fired through the open doorway.

One of the slugs smashed the flashlight in the hand of Karl Gardlund. The second knocked the light from Inspector Eames' grasp.

The two men retreated into the blackness to the awaiting posse at the edge of the bluff. No words were spoken and none were necessary, for they all realized their present situation. The show was over, their last hope was gone. It was now a matter of making a quiet exit. The discouraged party descended to the base of the bluff and the bank of the Rat River.

There was no alternative, with conditions as they were, except to return to Aklavik. But first the exhausted men had to have a brief period of sleep. Brush was thrown on the embers of the fire to bring a fleeting warmth, and, with two volunteers standing guard against any surprise attack from the Rat River Trapper, the rest of the posse, wrapped in their blankets, caught an hour's slumber around the campfire. Then the dogs were harnessed and the entire party set off for Aklavik.

From the top of the bluff, for the third time, Albert Johnson saw the Royal Canadian Mounted Police retreat before him.

CHAPTER ELEVEN

The Indian maid said, "I'll go with you
For I know how to handle a gun,
And when Mounties start closing in on you
You'll find two rifles better than one."

Again referring to the Toronto *Globe,* the issue of
January 19, 1932:

SIEGE OF MAD TRAPPER RESUMED
BY MOUNTIES

Strong Patrol Returns to Rat River, Where Constable's Assailant Still Defies Arrest In His Bomb-
Battered Cabin.

"Aklavik, N.W.T., Jan. 18: The Arctic was silent
tonight as the third act in a drama of the Northland
got under way. No word has been received of the
progress of the third Royal Canadian Mounted Police
patrol, headed by Inspector A. N. Eames, which
sought the arrest of Albert Johnson, a Rat River
trapper, barricaded in his cabin dugout on the old
Dawson Trail, 80 miles south of here.

"Johnson is sought for the shooting of Constable
A. W. King on Dec. 31, when the constable sought to
question him with regard to trapline interference.

Constable King suffered a serious wound from which he is recovering. On Jan. 10 the wanted man withstood a fifteen-hour siege by a second patrol which peppered his cabin with rifle fire and blew the top away with high explosives.

"The patrol returned to Aklavik, arriving Tuesday, to outfit for a third dash to the shack, and, if necessary, hold a longer siege. The larger force left this outpost within the Arctic Circle on Saturday, and will make every effort to capture the gunman.

"It is believed that Johnson, thinking he killed King, is prepared to resist capture to the limit."

As wires continued to crackle their ever more startling reports to the outside world, the North American public was gradually made aware of the grim tragedy being enacted in the silent Arctic. For the forces of law and order were not only being held in check, they were even being obliged to retreat before the blazing guns of one determined and solitary man.

It was unbelievable. Nothing like it had ever happened before.

As the days continued to pass and police posses knew further defeats, as another Mountie fell before the man with the hungry gun, an atmosphere of terror grew within the Arctic Circle. The February 2, 1932, issue of the *Globe* reported:

Fear is prevalent around the tiny post of Aklavik in the north-west corner of the North-West Territories, and tonight Aklavik is a haven for most of the women-folk in the district. Their husbands, who live by trapping, are all heavily armed and are assisting the police in their search for the fugitive. So at night the wives come in to Aklavik, fearful that the Rat River Trapper will come to their cabins when they are alone.

And mothers in the Northland began to silence their naughty children with "Hush, or the Rat River Trapper will get you."

So it is understandable, as reports from the Arctic began to appear almost daily in the press, that the public interest grew. Then radio commentators started to relate the latest news from the frozen north. The name of Albert Johnson, the Rat River Trapper, gradually became familiar to millions, both in Canada and the U.S. Radio announcers referred to the outbreak as the Arctic Circle War.

Yet it is doubtful that, in his shattered cabin near the Rat River, Albert Johnson was aware of his notoriety.

Inspector Eames and his half-frozen posse had arrived back in Aklavik on January 12, after their unsuccessful siege of the cabin.

With his usual thoroughness, Eames wasted no time in starting preparations for another assault. Two days later he dispatched Constable Edgar Millen back to the Rat River with orders to camp two miles from Johnson's cabin. He was to make no effort to apprehend the wanted man—merely to watch from afar, see if Johnson was still in his cabin, and observe his movements. Millen was accompanied by trapper Karl Gardlund.

On January 16, Eames set out with a second party in another attempt to capture Johnson. This group consisted of Constable Sittichiulis, ex-Constable John Parsons, Quartermaster Sergeant R. Riddell, trappers

Ernest Sutherland, Noel Verville, and Frank Carmichael, and Staff Sergeant H. F. Hersey.

Upon reaching the mouth of the Rat River, Eames recruited eleven Louchoux Indians who were camped near by. With a posse now nineteen strong, a camp was set up nine miles above the cabin. A severe windstorm which had raged for three days obliterated all tracks.

Constable Millen and trapper Gardlund arrived at camp with dismaying news. Albert Johnson had left his cabin. Two days earlier the Rat River Trapper had taken his departure and his present whereabouts was unknown.

Logic alone had caused Albert Johnson to forsake his battered cabin on the bluff. Following the latest withdrawal of the police posse, he was quick to realize that, though victory had been his, other posses—larger and better equipped, with more dynamite—would continue to come, again and again, until his fortress finally crumbled.

When daylight finally broke, around 11:00 a.m., he could see the damage the explosives had caused and he knew that his victory had been a costly one. There was a large hole in the roof, big enough for a man to crawl through. The window was shattered by rifle fire, while the heavy door was wobbly and hung at a crazy angle.

He set about repairing the door first, and finally had it back in position, though minus much of its former strength. Several food crates provided the wood to be nailed over the window opening.

But Albert Johnson made no attempt to repair the roof. With his heavy clothing and the fireplace blazing, he had no worry from the bitter cold, and why bother to patch up a roof that the next dynamite charge would again blast apart? There were other matters of more importance. First he would eat well, allow himself a two-day rest, and prepare for his departure.

When darkness fell on the third night, warmly apparelled, heavily armed, his trail-pack bulging with provisions and his hip-pockets with banknotes, he would disappear into the shadows. Yes, and he would be several long marches on his way before the police returned.

Furthermore, he had a set destination in mind. He realized that having shot an officer of the R.C.M.P. meant that he could never hope for peace as long as he remained in Canada. So there could be but one solution. He would travel west and make his way to Alaska.

True, such a decision meant a journey, alone and on foot, of over three hundred miles, and under the most cruel travelling conditions this world has to offer. Giant and jagged mountains lay between, and seemingly endless wastes of snow-covered tundra. The icy winds from the Arctic Ocean would be howling. The thermometer would stay at fifty below. Starvation would be a constant threat as posses of Mounties with ready rifles followed his trail.

Ah, but he knew that the R.C.M.P. could not follow him across the line that divided the bleak wastes of the Yukon from the equally bleak wastes of Alaska. Once in Alaska, he knew it would take months for United States officers to organize a posse and get into the Alaskan wilds to locate him.

But long before that happened, if we are to believe trapper George Case, he intended to be thousands of miles from North America. Case recalled:

"Once he had claimed the money he had in-herited—which had been waiting for him for years in the States—I think he planned to go away to the South Seas and live on some lonely island. Like a shipwrecked castaway. Oh he didn't come right out and say it in so many words, but there was no need to. I sensed it."

So it came about that on the third night following the siege, and after the last hot and hearty meal he would know for many days, Albert Johnson was ready to start.

He had made his preparations carefully and over-looked nothing. His trail-pack was filled with pro-visions carefully chosen for the precarious days ahead. And, of course, he also had his precious boxes of kidney pills.

For weapons he would carry his reliable 99 Savage .30-30 rifle, as well as a .22 Winchester rifle, model 58 with a cut-down stock. Then, since the occasion could arise when a police posse might be within close range, he decided to take along also his sawed-off 16-gauge shotgun. What became of his two automatic revolvers was never learned, though the police later searched the cabin and the surrounding area for the weapons. But they did come upon a carefully con-cealed food cache three hundred yards from the shack.

His leaving in the darkness of night was not without good reason. It was possible that unseen eyes could have been watching him from afar, during the hours of daylight.

He was in the act of reaching for the heavy trail-pack he would strap across his shoulders, when he paused for a final glance at the flames in the fireplace.

There had always been something about a fire that fascinated him. Watch the flames long enough, and they seemed to become as living things, mutely leaping upwards as they sought to convey some message of great importance to his ears. The thought might have come to him that it could be a long time before he would see another fire of his own making. So it would be best if he were to——.

What was that? Suddenly he had heard it. A faint sound that tensed him to rigidity.

Since he was about to take his departure, he had not bothered to barricade the door. But now, outside in the snow, he could hear the soft tread of running footsteps, making no more noise than the quietest whisper. Then, just beyond the door, the heavy breathing of one who has travelled far and fast. He silently reached for his rifle and watched the catch on the door slowly rise from the lock.

His gun-finger tightened on the rifle trigger as the door was gradually pushed inward and the cold wind whistled into the cabin. The next minute a rifle appeared, and then the one who carried it.

Anu, the Indian maid of Spatsizi.

"I thought it likely that you would be asleep," were her first words, "and I entered quietly as I did not want to disturb you. I could have kept watch till you awoke. And vigilance is important, since less than three miles from here, two white men—a Mountie and a trapper—have set up camp and are waiting for the moment when they can either shoot or capture you.

"My brother told me of their arrival some hours ago, and I passed within a short distance of their camp on my way here. But have no worry. The strong

blizzard that has started will have covered my footprints by now."

She closed the door and laid her rifle against the
wall. He could see the trail-pack strapped to her
shoulders.

He spoke at last: "They might have heard you."

"There is a saying among the people of my land,"
she replied with a smile. "You know the sun is in the
sky because you can see it. Also, you know a wolf
pack is near because you can hear its howls. But when
you see nothing and hear nothing, it's a Spatsizi
Indian."

She walked over to the fireplace, removed her
heavy mitts, and extended her hands towards the
flames.

"I have brought rations as well as my brother's
rifle and seventy rounds of ammunition. When the
next police posse comes, we can make our stand here
and we will fight them till the death."

Not till then did Anu notice that the other was
ready for flight. But then a look of understanding
crossed her face, and her eyes widened in happy
realization.

"You have finally decided to take my advice and
get away from this death-trap. Is that not so?"

He nodded.

"Good. The storm outside is certain to last for at
least two days and will hide our footprints almost as
fast as we make them. When the police get here we
will have had a start of several days and they will have
no idea as to where to begin their search. And no
knowledge at all of our destination."

For a long minute he looked at her. There was a
certain resignation in the voice of Albert Johnson
when he finally spoke:

"We are not going anywhere together. For me there must be no companionship. I regard such a desire as a sign of weakness. As long as I stay alive, I will stay alone."

In crushed silence she watched as he reached for his trail-pack. Next, two of his guns were secured to the trail-pack. He donned his heavy mittens and picked up his third weapon. He cast a final glance around the fortress he had built before turning again to her. For once his voice was gentle.

"Come, we will go now. I must head in the direction I have chosen and you can return to the cabin of your brother."

With that they walked out of the cabin and into the black Arctic night.

"I will take good care of your puppy. I promise I will."

Anu remained at the cabin of her brother till late spring, when she returned to her aunt in Aklavik.

After a year had passed, if we are to believe the story told of her, one day in the summer of 1933 Anu, with trail-pack strapped to her shoulders, began her long journey south to her homeland and parents. Just outside of Aklavik, she is said to have stopped before a certain tree where she remained for some time in agonized sorrow.

"If you had only listened to me. If you had only listened to me."

Finally, as a glance at the sky informed her that the day was advancing, Anu got to her feet and spoke to the young huskie dog that was her sole companion:

"We have many days to travel and must get started. At least in you I have something that was once his. Come on, Ace."

The tree she left behind her can still be seen today near Aklavik. A large "A.J." is carved in the trunk and at its base is a lonely grave.

CHAPTER TWELVE

"We'll meet again," Mountie Millen once told me.
"I'll be waiting for you," I had said.
So when he charged me with rifle blazing
I fired back and shot Millen dead.

With his nineteen-man posse encamped nine miles above the cabin of Albert Johnson, Inspector Eames heard the news of his flight with consternation.

Worse, there appeared to be no immediate way of learning the wanted man's whereabouts. The severe windstorm had lasted for the three days—January 16, 17, and 18—completely obliterating all tracks for miles around. So just where the posse should begin the search seemed to be anyone's guess. However, the shrewd Inspector Eames overlooked no possibilities: the large party, with the arrival of Millen and Gardlund now numbering twenty-one, fanned out along the Rat River canyon as far as the Bear River.

The possemen came upon a number of old cabins that had been erected years earlier, including the famous "haunted cabin" near the Bear River. It had been the scene of a brutal murder, and the former owner was said to return on the night of each anniversary of his cruel death to smoke his pipe in the very chair where he had been found with a knife in his back.

The posse also reported finding several of Albert Johnson's traplines, but there was no evidence of his having been there recently.

Right about then a crisis arose in camp. It was found impossible to keep so large a posse supplied with provisions and dog food. This was partly solved when Inspector Eames dismissed the eleven Louchoux. But there was also that matter of where to look next. Maybe it was instinct, maybe just a hunch, but after due consideration the Inspector formed the opinion that Albert Johnson had journeyed westward towards the Yukon. He decided to gamble on his theory and hand-picked a party for the venture.

The supplies on hand were checked and found to be enough to keep four men going for nine days.

Every one of those ten men had proved his worth in the bush. But Inspector Eames finally selected Constables Millen and Riddell and trappers Noel Verville and Karl Gardlund for the important assignment. The four were instructed to continue the search for Albert Johnson and travel to the west "as far as the Yukon Divide if necessary". They were also told that provisions would be hauled to the mouth of the Rat River for them, and that they would be relieved at the conclusion of nine days' search.

With that, Inspector Eames and the five other members of the posse returned to Aklavik, arriving there on January 23. As for the four who remained to continue the search, they had at least one way of keeping in contact. Constable Riddell was equipped with a portable short-wave transmitter and receiver, and was able to receive messages from Aklavik and occasionally transmit back.

Constable Millen and the three others, beginning near Albert Johnson's cabin, travelled west to the

Bear River, then went on into the high hills to the north of the river—a dreary area that seldom knew the tread of human footsteps. It was there, on January 28, that they met a Louchoux who had a trapline in that lonely district.

"Only yesterday I heard a shot of gunfire far to the west," he informed them. "I am sure it came from the rifle of the one you are seeking. The strange man with madness in his eyes who is known as Albert Johnson."

"You say you heard only one shot?" asked Constable Millen. "And what makes you so sure that Albert Johnson fired it?"

The Indian's answer was to the point.

"I know because Albert Johnson needs only one shot to kill anything he shoots at. If you ever get in front of his rifle, you will find that out for yourself."

The four men hurried westward. Of course there was always the chance that they were being led on a wild goose chase, but they decided to risk it. With nothing definite to work on, they could do little else. The recent windstorm had tossed the snow high and enabled them to use snowshoes, but even then their advance seemed woefully slow. They saw not the slightest evidence of any human presence. With the coming of night they made camp, but were up and on at daybreak. Around noon, chance brought them to a small creek. And it was there that they saw a trail of footprints.

Evidence also showed that the fugitive had camped near by on the previous night and could not be more than two hours ahead of them. The tracks were fresh.

The possemen sought out each other's eyes. They all realized that danger was ahead.

As rapidly as caution would allow, the men went forward, rifles ready, leaving nothing to chance. They were not blind to the possibility that the footprints might lead them into an ambush. Albert Johnson, aware of their approach, could be waiting ahead in some protected spot with his rifles and shotgun. However, this was a danger that had to be risked. They represented the law, and were there for the sole purpose of capturing one who had broken it.

The trail before them continued to stretch onward mile after mile, always to the west.

Its direct course finally caused Mountie Millen to comment. "I believe Inspector Eames had the right hunch. Albert Johnson is headed for the Yukon, though just how he thinks this can help him or what he hopes to find there is beyond me."

The trek continued on into the northern night. There was nothing but those tracks for the eye to see; and there had certainly been no sight of Albert Johnson, though the posse knew he was not far ahead of them. He seemed to be making no attempt to conceal his trail. His footsteps stood out in the snow with a clarity that a child could have followed.

"Something wrong here," was the opinion of Constable Riddell. "It's as if he were advertising his presence. As though he wants us to find him, and I don't like it. He's up to something."

That night camp was set up and rations slowly eaten by four uneasy men, who glanced frequently into the surrounding darkness. Riddell made a futile attempt to contact Aklavik on his short-wave transmitter. As the Arctic stars came out with their cold gleam a wolf-pack howled in the distance. Aware that vigilance must be maintained, the men took turns on lookout. There was no assurance that the Rat River

Trapper would not pay the camp a midnight visit and knife the lot of them.

With the coming of daybreak—January 30, 1932—the posse continued to follow the trail. Around noon, Constable Millen came to a stop and waved a mittened hand to bring the others forward. He pointed to a large and thick patch of timber ahead into which the footprints disappeared.

"He's in there, waiting for us. Somehow I feel it. It's our job to bring him out."

Slowly the posse crept forward, ready to answer any barrage of gunfire, till they reached the safety of the trees. Just a short distance within the trees began a long slope that led downward to a creek, a hundred yards away, and no search was needed to verify the presence of their quarry. For, as they stood there, from the creek below came a sudden loud and prolonged coughing.

The invincible Albert Johnson for some months had been tormented by violent coughing seizures that got worse and worse, and had reached the stage where he spat forth blood on the snow. Years of wandering the trails of the Arctic had taken their toll.

But his pursuers had to assume that his aim was still deadly. Keeping about twenty feet apart, they began a slow descent of the slope towards the creek, dodging from tree to tree. The coughing from below had stopped. They were still unaware of the exact location of the fugitive. Still hoping that the man could be apprehended without bloodshed, Constable Millen called out from the shelter of a spruce tree for Albert Johnson to surrender.

An immediate answer came from a thick patch of brush beside the creek at the bottom of the slope—a bullet plunged into the tree that shielded Millen.

As though at a signal, the four men stepped from the trees and fired blindly, sending some twenty bullets in all into the brush patch. As far as they could see, their shots only tossed up snow and brush-twigs. But the next moment they heard a loud and agonized cry from the bottom of the slope, followed by a violent thrashing in the thicket.

The last spasmodic convulsions of a dying man?

Then silence. A sepulchral stillness.

From the top of the slope, the four exchanged glances. Was this the end? Did it mean that Albert Johnson was dead? More silence. Then trapper Noel Verville, whose many years in the Northland had given him a thorough knowledge of both the wilderness and the men who lived there, called out softly:

"We better stay here for a while, Constable Millen, and see what happens. He could be hit, he might even be dead. But don't forget there is always the chance that he wasn't touched and just wants us to think he's dead. It's an old trick to get you to come closer. Yes, let's stay here for a spell."

The other agreed, and so the minutes passed. Twenty minutes. Forty minutes. Finally an hour. And during that time there was no suggestion of life from the brush patch. Neither the slightest sound or as much as the movement of a twig. At last convinced that Albert Johnson was either dead or unconscious, Millen told Gardlund and Verville to remain where they were and motioned to Riddell. The two Mounties, rifles before them, started to descend the slope toward the creek.

They did not get far—scarcely a matter of a dozen paces. For suddenly from the foliage the hungry gun of the Rat River Trapper blazed again. Constable

Edgar Millen was jerked half around before he crumbled limply to the snow. Dead almost instantly.

Hidden behind a large flat rock concealed in the centre of the brush patch, Albert Johnson had been safe from the fire of the posse. He had also feigned that cry and shaken the foliage to resemble the agonized thrashing of a dying man. Then he had patiently awaited developments. When Albert Johnson was fighting for his life, he fought no holds barred.

When Constable Millen fell to the snow, the three remaining possemen were appalled. Then implacably angry. Once again a shower of lead rained on the brush patch below, but crouched behind his shield the Rat River Trapper could ignore the bullets crashing and ricocheting against the rock.

As Riddell and Verville steadily poured bullets into the brush and prevented Albert Johnson from rising and returning the fire, Gardlund reached the dead body of Constable Millen, got it onto his powerful shoulders, and started hurrying up the slope to the bank and the timber beyond. It was an act of bravery worthy of the Victoria Cross.

Once Gardlund had disappeared over the top of the slope, Riddell and Verville, firing, slowly withdrew from tree to tree. When they finally were able to join Gardlund it was confirmed that Constable Millen was beyond earthly help.

So it is a matter of record that around 1:00 p.m. on Saturday, January 30, 1932, from a thicket five miles from the mouth of a creek that empties into the Rat River a mile north of the Barrier River, Albert Johnson for the fourth time saw the police retreat before him.

CHAPTER THIRTEEN

Fighting Mounties on land, I could beat them.
I had proved it, much to their despair.
So they sought outside help and they got it:
Planes with bombs came at me from the air.

The February 3, 1932, issue of the Toronto *Globe*
carried this headline:

BOMB TRAPPER OUT, ARE FLYING ORDERS
TO HIS ATTACKERS.
POLICEMAN IN "WOP" MAY'S PLANE WILL
DROP EXPLOSIVES ON LAIR.

The killing of the popular Constable Millen blew the
lid off the usually placid Northland. In fact, the
murder shocked the entire country. With radio and
press commentators demanding the immediate
capture of the killer, there was scarcely a hamlet or
crossroads even in the most remote areas of Canada
that was not aware of the Rat River Trapper and his
hungry gun. Among the titles given to Albert Johnson
were "The Madman of the North", "The Attila of the
Arctic", and "The Sadist of the Snows".

Feelings throughout the country were so high, it is
said that a salesman for a large Ontario firm by the

name of Albert John Johnson was driven to drop the "Albert" from his name.

Early on the day of the fatal shooting, Inspector Eames in Aklavik had sent Staff Sergeant Hersey and Constable Sittichiulis on ahead to reinforce the party of Constable Millen. Travelling by dog-sled, they made good time. On the afternoon of the second day, with their goal drawing nearer, an oncoming figure in the distance caused both men to bring their dog-teams to a sharp halt and reach for their rifles. The two exchanged glances.

Was it possible that the advancing man was Albert Johnson himself?

It was not till the other drew closer that they recognized their fellow officer, Sergeant Riddell, and could discern that he was anything but jubilant. Riddell gave them the shocking news of Millen's death. Gardlund and Verville were still at the end of the patch of timber with orders to watch the movements of Albert Johnson but to make no attempt to attack.

The three decided it would be best for Riddell, accompanied by Sittichiulis, to continue to Aklavik with news of Millen's death, while Hersey resumed his journey to the site of the killing and joined Verville and Gardlund.

Captain W. R. "Wop" May, Canada's famed pilot, flew his bomb-loaded plane more than a thousand miles from Edmonton to Aklavik to aid in the hunt.

An acclaimed hero of World War I, he became well known as a pioneer bush pilot in the far north, flying air-mail routes over formerly isolated areas, some of which extended to the shores of the Arctic Ocean.

Only two years before joining in the search for Albert Johnson, May's services had been invaluable in the discovery of the Colonel C. D. MacAlpine party, which had been lost on the bleak shore of the Arctic for two months.

Make no mistake about it. When it came to conducting an air search in the barren north for the tracks of a desperate fugitive, a more competent and experienced flyer than Captain Wop May would have been hard to find. May was like an eagle on the trail. One who followed tirelessly. One who would suddenly appear from out of the blue, swoop low as the wanted man made his way across a tundra or up a mountain trail, then hurry off to inform the police posses.

But May was to learn that searching for Albert Johnson was like trailing a phantom who could seemingly appear and disappear at will.

In Aklavik, it was a bitter Inspector Eames who listened as Sergeant Riddell told of the death of Constable Millen.

That same night the Inspector did something that was most unusual in the history of the Royal Canadian Mounted Police. Desperate in his attempt to cope with this threat to the peace of the Arctic, the Inspector made a public appeal over the local amateur broadcasting station at Aklavik. He asked for volunteers to assist the police in their search for Albert Johnson. At the same time, with the honesty that had won him the respect of so many, Eames informed them of the hardships and dangers such a venture might entail. He suggested that a decision to join the hunt should be pondered carefully.

The voice of the speaker reached the cabins of many who dwelt in lonely areas on the fringe of the

Arctic. A dreary world of snow, ice, and howling winds, and yet a world whose inhabitants were averse to bloodshed and murder.

The response to the appeal of Inspector Eames was prompt. From south, east, and west they came, an unkempt brigade of the brave, bewhiskered trappers, hunters, and prospectors. They came trooping into Aklavik, armed, grim, and fearless, with only one thought in their minds:

"Kill, get that murdering son of a bitch!"

Needless to say, Inspector Eames had little trouble in organizing another posse: when he again set forth from Aklavik, behind him were twelve seasoned veterans who were willing to follow him anywhere. Sergeant Riddell. Constables Hatting, Sittichiulis, Ethier, and Blake. Trappers Sutherland, Strandberg, Maring, Lange, Carmichael, Tardiff, and Greenland.

There went with them one more man—one willing to share the hardships and dangers of the others—the Reverend Thomas Murray. But he carried a cross instead of a rifle.

Eames and his posse left Aklavik on February 4, their immediate destination being the timber patch where Hersey, Verville, and Gardlund awaited their arrival. But before they completed their journey, as they neared the Rat River, they were overtaken by a messenger from Aklavik with heartening news: an airplane had been sent from Edmonton to assist them in their search, piloted by none other than the famous Captain "Wop" May. The posse cheered.

Late on the afternoon of February 5, the party reached the timber patch. And it was there that the awaiting Hersey, Verville, and Gardlund told Inspector Eames how Albert Johnson had done it again.

Two nights earlier, despite all precautions of the three watchers, he had quietly stolen away. Worse, since he had seemingly taken to the high ground, there was no evidence of his tracks and his present whereabouts was unknown.

But Eames was not worried. He knew that from here on in it would be only a matter of time.

True, the fugitive was utterly fearless, had a constitution of steel, was a dead shot with a rifle, and was undoubtedly experienced in all the tricks of trail-travel. Yet, at the same time, the Inspector remembered that Albert Johnson was human. He was not immune to the cold or to the gnawing pangs of hunger. And he could hardly afford the time to hunt while in flight. After a while his strides would become shorter and slower; exhaustion would claim him as it would anyone else. For nothing can take the spirit from a man as well as the strength from his body more surely than punishing days of Arctic travel— alone, on skimpy rations, and unable even to risk a campfire.

Two members of the posse returned to Aklavik with the body of Constable Millen.

The following day the other fifteen men searched the area surrounding the timber patch. A nine-mile ravine offered numerous hiding places where a harassed man might seek at least a temporary respite, but the area was given a thorough scrutiny and revealed no sign of the fugitive. They were now among a series of foothills that contained numerous ravines, creeks, and canyons. Ceaseless strong winds had scoured away all but the hard-packed snow.

Next day, February 7, the party came upon something that caused the heart of every man to beat faster: freshly made tracks that could only have been made by Albert Johnson.

More tracks were located in no fewer than three different creeks, two or three miles apart. They showed that the fugitive, travelling rapidly with his customary long strides, had been moving westward from creek to creek. However, the eagerness of the posse was squelched when they realized that they had been led in a ten-mile circle back to the very spot they had started from. Albert Johnson had seemingly vanished into thin air. They were left standing there, on the frozen Barrier River, totally bewildered.

Then a sudden droning in the sky drew their eyes up to the approaching plane of Captain May, who on sighting them landed on the tundra half a mile away. May had brought along Constable William Carter from Edmonton to join the searchers. Also, prior to landing he had seen a long trail of tracks that began several miles away and went westward. Albert Johnson was undoubtedly headed for the Yukon.

May's presence that night at the encampment caused quite a stir. Of course, the men had all heard of him and his exploits, but only Inspector Eames and two others had seen him before. Eames and May decided that the latter would bring in supplies from Aklavik for the posse, as well as feed for the ever-hungry huskies. Provisions and dog food, long the principal concern of police posses in the wilds, would no longer be a problem. May could also keep the posse informed of the whereabouts of the fugitive and the trails he had chosen.

When the men finally wrapped up in their sleeping blankets that night, it seemed to be the general opinion that the big difficulty had been hurdled. The rest would be but a matter of time as they pressed hard on the trail. Yes, only a few more days to go till Albert Johnson would be either a prisoner or a corpse.

Shortly after daybreak on the following morning, May's plane took off for Aklavik.

Several miles away a pair of hard and narrowed eyes watched his flight from the shelter of a snow mound.

Albert Johnson needed no two guesses to realize the purpose of that plane. From now on he would be hunted not only on the ground but from the air as well. Still another devil's creation to impede his journey, and there was such a vast distance to travel before he would reach the safety of the Alaska boundary.

Already ten days on the trail, the Rat River Trapper was far from pleased by his progress. To be sure, so far he had been careful; his long and circling trails had baffled his pursuers. A necessary precaution, of course, but time-consuming. In all, he was actually only a little more than a hundred miles nearer to his goal. There was still over two hundred to go—the breadth of the rugged Yukon, across the Yukon Divide.

No man, alone and in the dead of winter, had ever crossed the Yukon Divide. So Albert Johnson would have to be the first.

As he stood there watching the plane disappear, he was forced to acknowledge the terrible disadvantage to which it had reduced him in this grim game of hide-and-seek. The plane would fly in the best of supplies for the search parties, who could eat heartily and enjoy the warmth of a roaring fire. The plane could maintain their strength and add to it as necessary.

As for Albert Johnson, his circumstances were the direct opposite. There was not one comfort or aid he could look forward to. Just the cold, the snow, and the ice. Several times, he had been tempted to knock over a caribou and enjoy a steak feast. But caution always halted him: the report of a rifle, the light of a fire would betray him. He would have to subsist on the frozen rations he carried in his trail-pack, which was becoming ever lighter.

As he turned to continue on his way, he was suddenly gripped by another coughing seizure. A bad one this time. His rifle dropped as he struggled for breath. Invisible bands of iron seemed to be tightening around his chest and crushing him to death. When it finally passed, he swayed, weak and gasping. The world swam before his eyes. Once more there was blood on the snow.

For the Rat River Trapper was no longer his old robust self. His once hard and muscular frame was now fifteen pounds lighter. His every footstep was becoming an ordeal. But Albert Johnson was still alive and had yet to be beaten by any man.

And he was firmly determined to reach Alaska.

CHAPTER FOURTEEN

My past remains locked up within me.
There are secrets that I'll never tell.
Men who sought to learn them soon discovered
They had bought one-way tickets to hell.

"I believe I knew Albert Johnson better than any man in the north country," former trapper George Case once told me. Case was born with itchy feet and admitted to having "flung away nearly thirty years of my life chasing rainbows". He first met Albert Johnson in the summer of 1924 near Anyox, British Columbia.

"I wasn't any too flush with funds at the time, and I'd been working in the quartz mines at Anyox for a spell while I waited for something better to turn up. It finally did—I got lucky in an all-night poker session with three big-spending hunters from across the border. I made enough to buy a new outfit and head back north."

During the years that have passed since the February day in 1932 that witnessed the end of the Rat River Trapper, the stories told of him have become legion. Many are undoubtedly sheer fiction.

Stories that shatter like glass upon investigation, and are usually told by habitual tale-tellers. But there are other stories about the man that cannot be disproved. The story of George Case would seem to be one of them.

During his stay in Anyox in 1924, Case and four other workers in the quartz mines were staying at the home of an enterprising housewife who ran a boarding house where smiles were few and luke-warm hash frequent.

Then one day a stranger drifted into the small settlement, a man with stern, swarthy features and hard eyes. He had taken possession of a deserted cabin a mile or so from the village. He rarely spoke to anyone and seldom left his cabin except to walk into Anyox for supplies.

"Several times I saw him pass the house where I was staying," Case recalled. "He would be going to and from Anyox and always walked briskly with eyes front. We wondered who he was and where he came from, but nobody wanted to question him.

"One Sunday I was out for a walk, and was passing his cabin when I stopped to light a cigar. Then I noticed him standing in the doorway about ten yards off the road. When I had got my cigar going, I said:

" 'A birthday present I bought for myself, since no one else would buy me one.' With that I pulled a second cigar from my coat pocket and offered it to him. But he shook his head. Then I told him I had come into the world thirty years ago that day, and all I had to show for it was the gold in my teeth. And then an odd thing happened, because he suddenly seemed to be paying attention to me.

" 'You have gold dental work in your mouth?' he said. 'Do you?'

"But I shook my head and told him it was just a joke. No, I had no gold in my teeth, or in my pockets for that matter, and right then I didn't see that I possibly ever would.

"At that he seemed to lose interest in me—he just turned and disappeared inside his cabin. So I went on with my walk. But I couldn't help but wonder why he had asked such an odd question, and he seemed so serious about it. As if it was a matter of life or death. It was not till years later that I heard those other stories, and when I did I went weak in the knees. I realized I had been scant inches from the old gent with the scythe."

A short while later Albert Johnson vanished from the Anyox area, and scarcely a month more had passed before George Case had the lucky poker session that permitted him to buy a new outfit and head north to resume trapping.

The result was that mid September of 1924 found Case in a cabin somewhere in the vast territory between Dease Lake and Teslin Lake in northern British Columbia, less than fifty miles south of the Yukon border. Practically isolated from the rest of the world, Case laid out his traplines and looked forward to a remunerative if lonely winter. But he soon learned that he had a neighbour. One day only a few weeks after his arrival, as he explored his surroundings about five miles west of his cabin and mulled over the possibilities of running another trapline, Case topped a ridge and beheld a small cabin scarcely a hundred yards ahead.

It had probably been erected by some wandering trapper or prospector, or perhaps even by some hardy sons of the Yukon's gold-rush days. Hundreds of similar cabins can still be found throughout northwestern Canada today, their original owners long forgotten.

However, it was immediately evident that this particular cabin was not deserted. Some recently cut firewood was stacked near the door, a curl of smoke rose from the chimney, and a canoe was pulled up on the bank of the creek. But, as he drew closer, Albert Johnson suddenly appeared from the rear of the cabin with rifle in hand.

"Who are you and what do you want?"

George Case has told me: "I sure was surprised to see him. I walked forward, called out hello, and said: 'Remember me? I met you near Anyox, about three months ago. The sixth of June, my birthday. But you were more interested in finding out if I had any gold in my teeth. So I'll tell you again. I'm as free of gold as a frog is of feathers.' "

But Albert Johnson was in no mood for frivolities; he immediately ordered Case to be on his way. As Case, somewhat bewildered, turned to go, behind him he could hear the other mumbling, "Fools coming into my territory, who have nothing better to do than to wander around and disturb a man's privacy."

Case turned back at this:

"I'm sorry if my being in your territory disturbs you, but I wasn't aware that you owned British Columbia. And I'm not exactly treading on your heels. My cabin is five miles away."

"Then go to your cabin and stay in your cabin. Better still, when you get there, hang yourself. Come this way again and I'll see to it that pieces of you wind up in the guts of a wolf pack."

George Case was a well-built man, unusually muscular, and certainly no coward. He proved as much, time and again in his thirty years in the Northland. But he was also a tactful man and realized that the present occasion was not one for anger. So he made no reply and continued on his way.

On two occasions during the following three months, Case saw his mysterious neighbour from a distance, evidently returning home after an inspection of some trapline. Both times Case went to the door of his cabin, waved, and called out a greeting, but the other made no response. He would just give him an indifferent glance and resume his journey.

Finally, as Christmas drew near, Case journeyed on snowshoes to a trading store near Dease Lake, thirty miles to the south-east. There he purchased some needed items for the days ahead. And it was there that the trader, who had known him in former days, asked Case if he knew an Albert Johnson who was trapping in the district "north-west of the Dease and somewhere around your territory".

Case nodded and said that Albert Johnson lived practically next door.

"He came in here about five weeks ago and asked for six boxes of kidney pills," said the trader. "I told him I was out of them and didn't expect to get any more till after the New Year. But a supply arrived only a few days ago, and if you see him you can tell him I have them. Better still, you could take them to him yourself, as he seemed anxious to get them."

Case agreed. Then a sudden thought came to him.

Trading stores carried just about everything one needed for survival in the harsh north. From traps, guns, and ammunition to clothing, medical aids, and hard candy. Case finally found what he sought: a heavy blue woolen shirt and a pair of equally heavy socks. He asked: "Can you wrap them up in something fancy? Put some green or blue ribbon around it and make it look like a Christmas gift?"

He arrived back in his cabin on December 24.

The following day around noon—Christmas Day, 1924—he was about ready to journey the five miles to the home of his neighbour when he looked out from his cabin and saw the man himself in the distance. Case shouted to him, telling him of the kidney pills he had brought from the trading store. Reluctant as well as suspicious, Albert Johnson finally came forward and entered the cabin.

"He even stayed and had Christmas dinner with me," Case recalled. "It took a lot of coaxing, of course, and he wasn't exactly bubbling over with the spirit of Yuletide. He rarely spoke, but I think he enjoyed himself. As for the shirt and pair of socks I had bought for him, he said it was the first Christmas present he'd got in many years."

During the following seven months, Case made a point of visiting the cabin of Albert Johnson for brief visits every few weeks. True, his host did not welcome him with smiles and open arms. In fact, he rarely spoke. But he no longer threatened to feed him to the wolves. From the odd word dropped here and there, Case pieced together the information that Albert Johnson had been born near Bismarck, North Dakota, in 1897. Case himself was a native of Manitoba, which borders North Dakota.

Case said once: "In view of what happened, I am certain that his parents were wealthy and left him a fortune." He then explained:

"I remember the time when I happened to speak of the Indian who stopped off at my cabin a few days earlier and said that the price of pelts had taken a sharp drop. 'If it's true, it will raise hell with the trappers,' I told Johnson. 'It means we'll all have to worry about money.' And he said:

" 'It will mean nothing to me. I've never had to worry about money in my life and never will. My mother saw to that.' "

About two weeks after Johnson made the above remark, Case opened his cabin door one morning to discover a strip of birch-bark on which were scrawled the words: "Go to cabin. Take what is there." Concerned, Case hurried to the cabin to find it deserted. On a small table Case found what its former tenant had purposely left behind him—a number of pelts that would bring good prices.

They represented the fur catch of Albert Johnson during the past eight months.

"He must have remembered what I'd said about the drop in fur prices. He didn't need the money, so he left his whole catch of skins for me. Yes, and when you got to know the man you could expect something like that. He hated to see anybody or anything left weak and helpless.

"He would even feed young animals—I've often seen a flock of them around his door.

"Again, on other occasions, he could be unbelievably cruel. But don't ever think for a minute that he was crazy. It was just that the world didn't understand him. He only wanted to be alone. Put him on a large and deserted island with only animals and birds for company and he would have been a happy man."

More than a year passed. Then, one fall day in 1926, far to the north of Hazelton, somewhere around the Stikine River district, George Case saw Albert Johnson again. Case and a fellow trapper named Joe LaBelle, on their way to a Hazelton trading store to sell their furs, had paused on the trail for flapjacks and a cup of tea when the Rat River Trapper appeared from a near-by woods and came forward. Case waved a hand and asked him to join in the meal.

Albert Johnson nodded and unstrapped his trail-pack, laying his rifle across it.

"He hardly spoke, he ate in silence, and I knew better than to ask him a lot of questions," Case related. "Frankly, I think that was the reason why he could tolerate me. I never got too curious and I made it a point to limit my words. For if there was one thing that infuriated Albert Johnson, it was a talkative man. Nor did I make any mention of the furs he had left for me in his cabin. I knew he wouldn't like it.

"When he finished his flapjacks and tea, Johnson got to his feet, picked up his pack and rifle, nodded to me, then began a brisk walk to the north-west. LaBelle and I went on south towards Hazelton. And that night, before the campfire, LaBelle told me he had seen Johnson before. Two years earlier in Kamloops, someone had pointed out Johnson to him as the man who had damn near beaten two husky trappers to death with his bare fists."

According to LaBelle, in the summer of 1922, in one of the wild mountainous areas back of British Columbia's Kis-Ki-Gas and Nil-Kit-Gas rivers, two trappers had shot a small fawn barely old enough to walk and unsteady on its legs. Of course it was a cruel thing to do, but the two seem to have been a heartless pair. Then as they gathered around their kill, a stranger had appeared from a near-by patch of dense timber. And when he had taken in what had happened, he'd said, very calmly:

"I'm going to beat the two of you into butchered, bleeding hamburger."

Then, leaning his rifle against a tree and whisking off his jacket, he proceeded to do just that. Both of them were brawny fellows, handy with their fists, but they did not have a chance against him. He had the strength of a maniac. Snarling like a wildcat, his slashing fists smashed to the guts, the groin, the face, too fast for any defence.

"He was like something that lived in a cave a million years ago. And he never stopped that animal-like snarling. Finally he had the both of them on the ground, bleeding and unconscious. Then he put the boots to them and broke several of their ribs. Also the jaw of one of them.

"Now, you would have thought he should have been satisfied. But he wasn't. Not him. Instead, he stood there and waited till they came to themselves, and, though they both begged for mercy, he yanked them to their feet and once more beat them senseless. Then, when they were finally so messed up their own mothers wouldn't have recognized them, he broke their rifles on the trunk of a tree and left."

CHAPTER FIFTEEN

So on that distant day my quest started,
As I searched for that killer and thief.
And I only had one clue to go on:
Find a man who had gold in his teeth.

"After we met on the trail that day, nearly two years passed before I saw Albert Johnson again," said George Case. "My partner Joe LaBelle and I had worked our way north into the Yukon Territory. We spent the winter of 1927 around the Pelly River and by midsummer had ourselves a prime catch of hides. So we went to Mayo to sell the pelts, got a good price, and had a week's fling.

"We returned by way of Fraser Falls, as Joe had a girl—a trapper's daughter—who lived with her parents only a few miles from there. But I figured the cabin would be crowded enough without me, so I told Joe I would go on to the Falls and pick him up in the morning. Well, I got to Fraser Falls, walked into Bob Levac's trading store and hadn't been there five minutes when in comes Albert Johnson. I learned he had arrived there twenty-four hours earlier and had rented a small cabin behind the store for a few days.

"I asked if he could put me up for the night. He stared at me for a moment, then finally nodded.

"That night Johnson was his usual moody self. He neither smoked or drank, you know, but he didn't object to my having a cigar and seemed interested in the smoke-rings I blew at the ceiling. He finally commented:

" 'Like life, they fade to nothing and are forgotten.'

"Later that night he did talk a bit more. There was a book in the cabin, an old and battered copy of the one about that fellow who lived alone on an island for so many years. I picked it up and I said: 'Did you know that Defoe got his idea for this story from a sailor who was actually marooned on an island for years? The fellow's name was——'

" 'Selkirk.' He was almost shouting. 'And like all humans, Selkirk was an ass. The man had a tropical paradise, away from the rest of the world. He was the nearest to heaven he could ever hope to get in this life, but lacked the brains to realize it. He finally left the island. Yes, the man was a fool.'

"That was the end of his talking for that night."

George Case and Joe LaBelle returned to their cabin near the Pelly River, where they carried on with their trapping for nearly three years. From their viewpoint it was a profitable period but a lonely one, interrupted only by the occasional trapper or prospector who came their way and paused to relate the latest news of the outside world. Then, in the early spring of 1931, Case and LaBelle travelled east to fresh territory.

April found them in a cabin near a creek in Northwest Territories about twelve miles east of the Yukon Divide. They looked forward to another profitable year.

"And we hadn't been there more than three weeks when one morning who should come along but the wandering Albert Johnson. As usual, he carried his rifle and trail-pack and was probably going, like he once told me, to where the wind would take him. So I asked him in for a meal.

"I heated him up some rabbit stew, laid the plate on the table before him, threw down the tools, then sat back to watch him eat. He always did the same thing. He laid the knife on the right side of the plate, the fork on the left, and set down the dessert spoon straight across the top. The way they do it in society. Of course there was no dessert, but that's the way he did it and it told me plenty.

"Albert Johnson must have been used to the finer things in life—servants, cars, fancy hotels, and such. Born with a silver spoon in his mouth.

"When he finished his meal, he rose, gave me a nod of thanks, took up his pack and rifle, and departed. He had completely ignored Joe LaBelle the whole time. After he left, I turned to Joe and said: 'He's a strange man, that Albert Johnson. A mystery if there ever was one.'

" 'I don't think a hell of a lot of your friend,' was Joe's answer.

" 'Why didn't you tell him that to his face when he was here?'

" 'Because he would have shot me dead in my tracks. I tell you, that fellow is a killer. I can see it in his eyes.' "

Eight more months passed. Life went on as usual for George Case and Joe LaBelle. Then, one day shortly after the New Year in 1932, an Indian hunter stopped off at their cabin to tell them the news that had the

entire Arctic in a frenzy of excitement. Near the
distant Rat River, a trapper had shot a Mountie. Not
only that, when Inspector Eames had arrived at the
trapper's cabin with a posse, the trapper had held
them off for fifteen hours and the police were finally
obliged to retreat.

And the name of the trapper? The Indian knew.
The man's name was Albert Johnson.

"When the Indian mentioned the name," recalled
George Case, "Joe LaBelle just turned and gave me
one of his I-told-you-so looks."

More weeks passed. On two other occasions,
travellers had stopped to tell them further news—the
manhunt was on.

Then came February 8, 1932, the most memorable
day in Case's life.

"Joe LaBelle was away and I did not expect him back
for at least three more days. He'd gone to Aklavik
with some pelts and was going to get some supplies.

"Well, early on the morning of February 8, two
trappers with rifles and dog-teams stopped off at the
cabin long enough to warm themselves and have a cup
of tea. They were members of a posse that was
searching for Albert Johnson, and were separated
from their party which was camped eighteen miles to
the north-east. Johnson had shot down and this time
killed another Mountie and was still on the loose.

"They told me about Inspector Eame's radio
appeal, and that Captain May was hunting for tracks
from the air. When they drove away, one of them
turned and called back to me:

" 'Wherever he is, Albert Johnson is a gone gosling
now. Hundreds of men are ready to blast him
apart.' "

Early that afternoon I heard a droning sound overhead, and came out to have a look. And there was May's plane. It would make a giant circle in the sky, then swoop lower. It was like watching an eagle about to make a kill.

"The rest of the day seemed to drag along, and when it got dusk I could see that we were in for a heavy snowfall.

"That night I sat staring at the fire, and I started thinking about some things I had heard about the 'Gold-Dust twins' from a trapper named Bradley. He also said he'd seen Albert Johnson in the area right around the time the two men had been murdered. I had also heard what the Netsilik Eskimoes called him, and a lot of other stories besides.

"But the idea of Albert Johnson taking gold teeth from dead bodies did not make sense. It was ridiculous. Johnson had no need for those bits of gold. Everybody knew he had ample money.

"But then, since I'd last seen him, he had shot two men. So for all I knew all the stories were true and he was a murder-mad lunatic.

"It must have been close to midnight when I finally put out my pipe and thought about bed.

"Then, by God, there was a knock at the door.

"For a minute I was too surprised to do anything but stand and gape. In the name of sanity, who could be abroad at such an hour and in the storm? Then the knocking came again, louder. So I did the only thing there was to do. I walked over to the door and there was Albert Johnson himself."

CHAPTER SIXTEEN

Go bring on your lawmen by the dozens.
They can be white, black, yellow, or brown.
And let them and their guns do their damnedest,
But I'll get some before I go down.

"You know something? Even after so many years, whenever I think of Albert Johnson I always picture him as he looked on that night.

"But when I first opened the door, he looked pretty much as he always had—same sort of clothes, same pack, same rifle. The same hard face.

" 'Come in,' I said. 'For God's sake come in quickly!'

"I closed and then barred the door behind him, then I asked: 'Do you think you have been followed? Are they on your heels? Of course you know they're out to get you.'

"He shook his head as he removed his trail-pack, hat, and parka, and said: 'You mean they're out to try and get me. This afternoon I shook them off. They're about fourteen miles north-east of here. They'll think I've headed south. But if they bring more men and planes, when it comes I'll just have to meet it. Nothing is going to stop me. I've decided that.'

" 'Where do you plan to go?' I asked.

" 'A long way from here,' was his answer.

"With that he walked over and sat down on the chair before the fire. Then he said: 'I'm tired, George. I'm very tired.'

"It was the first time he had ever called me by my name in all the years I had known him.

" 'You're hungry, of course.'

" 'Famished.'

" 'I'll damn soon take care of that.'

"So after I built up the fire, I grilled him a thick venison steak and heated up my last can of tomatoes.

"While he was eating, I got a good look at him. He was a good twenty pounds lighter and what he'd gone through in the last four weeks was right there on his face to see. The cold had got him, and hunger had got him, and if being hunted down hadn't got him it had come damn close.

"And then he started coughing. It went on about five minutes, with him just sitting there helpless, trying to smother it with a bandana. Once the spell was over he looked down at the bandana and said:

" 'It would seem that I have had enough of the Arctic and should make for a land of sunshine.'

" 'Like the fellow in Defoe's book who lived on an island and ate coconuts and bananas in his naked pelt?'

" 'Something like that.'

"Oddly enough, when he finished his meal and I was certain he would make for the bunk, he seemed to come to life again. He went back to the chair in front of the fire and he asked me to join him.

" 'Let's watch the fire for a while before we turn in,' he said. 'I love to see the flames. If you look at them long enough, you begin to think of earlier days, and what might have been. As for sleep, it is of no importance. It is merely a brief death!'

"I remember I got out my old reliable mouth organ and played several tunes. The truth is, I was rather proud of my ability with the instrument—still am—and I rattled off 'Casey Jones', 'Turkey in the Straw', 'Mrs. Murphy's Chowder', 'The Wreck of the Old 97' and the like. But I don't think he particularly liked that type of music. In fact, I know damn well that he didn't, for suddenly he said:

" 'Don't you know anything else but that bawdy bar-room trash?'

"I did and I told him I did. I said that I was not just the ordinary run-of-the-mill sort of mouth-organ player. That as well as playing jigs and reels I could also render the finer type of music. Classics and the like. Yes, and to prove it I played 'Just a Song at Twilight' and 'A Perfect Day'. Then I recalled a certain piece I had known since I was a boy. True, I couldn't remember the title but it was a beautiful melody. Sad and haunting. I put my all into it, and when I finished he had the strangest look in his eyes.

" 'That song. I know it,' he said. 'It was my mother's favourite and I have heard her sing it a hundred times. George, play it again. I remember the words and I want to sing it. Yes, play it again.'

"And don't think for a minute that Albert Johnson couldn't sing it. He had one of the finest baritones I have ever heard. He got up on his feet, and sang with me accompanying him, and he seemed to be not there at all but somewhere in the past.

> In the gloaming, oh my darling.
> When the lights are dim and low.
> And the quiet shadows falling,

Softly come and softly go.
When the winds are sobbing faintly,
With a gentle, unknown woe.
Will you think of me and love me,
As you did once long ago.

"I tell you, if you could have heard him you wouldn't believe that he was the one the police were after.

"When we had finished the song, he walked very slowly over to the bunk and took off his boots. Then he ran his hand through his hair and yawned. But then, as though struck by a sudden thought, his eyes went to me and he said:

"'George, how about heating up that teapot? I could use another cup, and it's been so long since I've been able to go to bed with a warm belly that I want to take advantage of it.'

"So I poured hot water from the grate into the pot and added more tea.

Now there was that one question in my mind and I just had to know the answer. So while we waited till the tea steeped, I came right out with it:

"'There have been several trappers dropping in here during the past two weeks, and all of them were talking about you. And they tell a lot of pretty hair-raising stories.' Then I stopped there, feeling like a damn fool.

"Albert Johnson took his tea and sat down again on the bunk. 'Get to the point, George. Get to the point and stop beating around the bush. What is it you want to say?'

"'Tell me, have you been roaming around the Arctic for years, killing men who had gold fillings in their mouth, then keeping the fillings? Have you?

And if so, why? For the love of God, why?'

"He never as much as flickered a muscle or showed the slightest emotion. Instead, he raised the cup to his lips and took several sips of hot tea. It was so quiet I could hear the ticking of the alarm clock. Finally he started talking, very quietly.

" 'I had a very unusual mother, George. One whose preferences for solitude and isolation were seemingly inherited by me. She was an artistocrat to her fingertips. She was wealthy, she was intelligent, and she was an outstanding beauty. I adored her. Then, when I was twenty and she was only thirty-eight——it was a great tragedy, George. Oh, I was not long in exacting vengeance, I assure you. I dealt with her destroyer in the manner he deserved. For your own sake, I will spare you the details.

" 'But she was gone and something in me was gone too. Without her, life was but a mockery, an agonized existence with neither reason nor purpose. I had to get as far away from all others as possible. And so, at twenty-one—fourteen years ago—I came north. But even here they have never left me alone.

" 'I have seen humanity around me, living their stupid existences. Faces like steers, laughing like idiots or smirking like fools. Repulsive lumps of flesh that walk and should never have been. I have asked myself over and over, what right has this scum to exist while the only one who meant anything to me was pushed into her grave? And I have the answer. The very existence of these people is an outrage against all that is just and decent. Mankind isn't worth a damn, should be smashed to nothing like a cockroach.'

"He finished his tea, and as he handed me the cup he added:

" 'Now, as for your question. You want to know if I have been roving over the Arctic killing men for the gold in their teeth. So I will give you my answer. I am going to let you figure that out for yourself, and when you have reached your decision you can keep it a secret. Even from me, George. Good night.'

"With that he lay back on the bunk, flung the sleeping blanket over him, and in three minutes was asleep."

"The following morning we were both up before 5:00. Daybreak wouldn't come before 11:00, and Albert Johnson could have a start of several hours on the trail before that.

"He ate a hearty breakfast with the calmness of a man who didn't have a care in the world—as though all he was going to do was sit down to a good book and a cigar in his favourite armchair in front of the fireplace. Not a nerve in his body.

"When he had finished his meal, he got to his feet, nodded his thanks to me, then without a word put on his parka and hat and strapped on his trail-pack. When he was eating I had slipped a few small items into the pack, but he was still badly provisioned for a journey of any distance. Next he secured his two guns to his pack and—would you believe it?—he was whistling to himself. The song he had sung the night before.

"He started towards the doorway, the 99 Savage .30-30 rifle in his right hand. Then a sudden thought seemed to strike him, for he stopped and asked: 'Do you need any money? Could you use a thousand dollars?'

" 'No, I'm making out all right. I've saved some money. Besides, you have already given me too damn much.'

"At the door he paused to lace on his snowshoes. When he rose and turned to me for the last time, he seemed to read on my face exactly what I was thinking, for he said:

" 'No. I won't be alone out there, I do have one friend who always comes to help me in time of peril. The spirit of my mother. Her voice comes to me on the wind. Lately I have been hearing her voice even on the cold wind from the Arctic Ocean. She awakens me and warns me when police posses are getting near. She is always with me now.'

"His eyes shone as though in triumph:

" 'So I'll still make it to where I am going, despite the police with their posses, guns, bombs, and planes. I cannot fail.'

"With that, Albert Johnson opened the door and walked into the darkness. He was still confident that he would get to wherever he was going. There is no doubt about it. For, as I stood there, feeling pretty shaky, he called back:

" 'See you later.' "

CHAPTER SEVENTEEN

Oh, I sure made those posses look foolish,
Many more times than they'd care to tell.
And as I fled over the wild mountains,
I out-foxed and out-shot them as well.

The morning of February 9, 1932, found Inspector Eames with a large posse of Mounties, trappers, and Indian guides encamped near the Barrier River in the north-west section of the Northwest Territories.

That it was a somewhat puzzled party of man-hunters, there can be little doubt. For days now they had been following Johnson's trail with notable lack of success. While the trails of the wanted man were numerous, they all apparently led to nowhere. The posse would follow tracks that went on for miles, only to find themselves led in a circle.

"We finally got to thinking that he could sprout wings and fly away whenever he wanted to," one of the men recalled in later years.

Even up in the sky Captain May was encountering nothing but frustration. Several times he had flown over the tracks only to find that they eventually led into some ravine or stretch of timber where they would abruptly disappear.

Once, near the Bell River, the flyer's hopes started to rise. He was following snowshoe tracks, momentarily expecting to come upon the fugitive himself. But the trail vanished in a long, wide, and recently made caribou trail. Albert Johnson had removed his snowshoes, and by walking on his heels had buried his footprints in a maze of caribou tracks that stretched both ways for miles.

And so the days went on, one by one, with Albert Johnson still at large and slowly but surely moving ever closer to the sanctuary of Alaska.

Unexpectedly, three possemen did come near to catching him—two trappers and an Indian, who had become separated from the main party. They caught a fleeting glimpse of the fugitive, far in the distance and hurrying westward. In the brief exchange of rifle fire that followed, one of the trappers received a severe shoulder wound that demanded the attention of his companions. Johnson continued on his way, still free and untouched.

On February 9, still another patrol joined the large posse of Inspector Eames near the Barrier River. The latest arrivals consisted of Constables Sidney Day and John Moses as well as two trappers and two Indians of the Yukon's Old Crow Detachment.

The next day, Constable Moses led a small patrol to as far as the last timber of the Barrier River.

It is a district of an unusual number of rolling hills, brooks, and ravines, and while it seemed unlikely that Johnson would be hiding in the area there was always a chance. And it was there that the patrol came upon an exciting discovery: a recently made snowshoe track, undoubtedly the trail of the wanted man, and headed towards the west. Directly west. But why? For what reason? To go west was to come upon the

Yukon Divide. The men turned to each other with the same question in mind.

Could it be that he was desperate enough to be actually thinking of trying to get over the Yukon Divide?

"It is impossible for anyone to cross the Yukon Divide, alone, in the dead of winter," Indians and trappers had told Inspector Eames. "It can't be done."

Deathly ill and half starved as he was, Albert Johnson, the Rat River Trapper, crossed the Yukon Divide alone and in the dead of winter. That is a matter of record. The sufferings he endured can only be speculated upon. But he did cross the Yukon Divide.

Inspector Eames received the surprising news late on the afternoon of February 12. It was brought by Peter Alexis, an Indian from the small settlement of La Pierre House in the extreme eastern section of the Yukon, not far from the Yukon Divide. Peter Alexis had asked to be taken directly to Inspector Eames.

The note he brought was written by Harry Anthony, a well-known Yukon trapper. It was brief and to the point. A wandering group of Indians had come upon a long and strange snowshoe track not far from La Pierre House. The description of the track was that of Albert Johnson.

Hoarse exclamations of surprise could be heard among the posse members when they learned that the fugitive was in the Yukon. He had given them the slip again and was now miles to the west. Not only that, perhaps even as they stood there he was increasing his lead on them. And it was obvious now that he was heading for some particular destination. But where?

For some days the far-thinking Inspector Eames had been aware that it might well be Alaska. And he could see only too well the inevitable delay of at least a few months, while American posses were organized and official documents put in order. Now, in view of the information he had just received, there would have to be a drastic change in plans.

Luckily, only a few minutes before the arrival of the Indian messenger, Captain May had landed his plane near by. In fact he had been conferring with Eames when Peter Alexis drove into the camp. After a few minutes' thought Eames called the members of the posse together to inform them what was to happen.

Eames, along with Sergeant Riddell and trapper Karl Gardlund, would be immediately piloted by Captain May to Aklavik.

It was of vital importance that the whereabouts of Albert Johnson be made known to the Aklavik broadcasting station without delay. Thus the scattered inhabitants throughout the large and rugged Yukon could be warned that the notorious killer was now in their territory, travelling westward.

On the following day—February 13—he, Riddell, and Gardlund would be flown over the Yukon Divide to La Pierre House.

The Inspector then chose eight men from the posse whose immediate services would be required in the Yukon: Constables Day, Moses, Sittichiulis, and Hersey, trappers Verville, Ethier, and Jackson, and the Indian messenger Peter Alexis. With the coming of daybreak, they were to hurry on by dog-team to La Pierre House by way of Loon Lake and Bell River, where the search would be continued. As for the other members of the posse, with the dawn they were to return to Aklavik and await further orders.

A short while later, Captain May took off for Aklavik with Eames, Riddell, and Gardlund.

That night the rest of the posse heard, on the portable short-wave receiver, the voice of the announcer from Aklavik warning the inhabitants of the Yukon that the "murdering madman of the Arctic" was now travelling through their territory in a westerly direction as he sought to reach Alaska, two hundred miles away.

"Take no chances with him for the man is extremely dangerous. He has already killed and will not hesitate to do so again. If you see signs that indicate his presence in your vicinity, notify the nearest authority as soon as possible. Housewives in isolated areas are asked to keep their cabins barred and bolted. Their husbands are urged to maintain a constant lookout for any approaching stranger."

CHAPTER EIGHTEEN

So across a frozen world I struggled.
It meant death if I were to fail.
And at nights I could see distant campfires
Of the Mounties who were on my trail.

On the morning of February 10, 1932, when Albert Johnson set foot in Yukon Territory with the pursuing police apparently far in the rear, he realized his last and final adventure was still before him—a rapid two-hundred-mile journey across the grim and desolate Yukon to Alaska.

He was anything but his former robust self. Exhausted and half-starved, he was losing weight rapidly. His pace was no longer the fast, swinging stride that had been so characteristic of him for years. Numerous halts were made necessary by his waning strength and violent coughing seizures.

But Albert Johnson's hopes were high. True, he realized he could not complete the journey as rapidly as he might have in former days. Also, he must proceed with extreme caution and might still be obliged to make some long and tiring circling manoeuvres to throw off the police. They might soon become aware that he was now in the Yukon and moving westward. But he still had his indomitable courage and spirit. And he still had his hungry gun. It would get him to his goal.

His former years of wandering had made him familiar with the territory, at least to the point of having a good idea of his present position. Far to the south-west he recognized the lofty mountain peak that stood out majestically watching the struggles of life in the world below. He could even make out the dark blotches of the patches of timber that studded the mountain and crowned its top. Yes, he would still make it to Alaska.

Several days passed during which his progress was uninterrupted. The Alaska border came steadily closer, and he knew the solitude he craved. True, on reaching the area around the Bell and Eagle rivers, he was obliged to lose considerable time in making circling manoeuvres and backtracks. But he knew it was a necessary precaution. And he could enjoy the frustration he was causing.

Then, on the afternoon of February 16, he topped a high elevation and found himself a scant half mile away from an occupied cabin.

As his tracks later indicated, he must have spent at least an hour, unseen, watching that cabin. Of course, by that time his trail-pack was empty of provisions. Why did he not go forward, shoot down whoever was inside, and take what he wanted? His cunning told him not to—if he did that he would be advertising his presence in the Yukon, and he had as yet seen nothing to suggest that this was even suspected. He wanted it to remain that way. Besides, with such a lead on his pursuers, it would soon be reasonably safe to risk not only the far-reaching report of a rifle but the comforting warmth of a campfire as well.

Yes, just a bit longer. Play if safe for another day. Then, food and warmth. Plenty of both.

Having reached his decision, he passed the cabin by. Once in Alaska he would find a cabin, stock it with provisions, and sleep for a week before a roaring fire.

On February 13, Inspector Eames, Sergeant Riddell, and Karl Gardlund were flown over the Yukon Divide to La Pierre House.

As his coming had been announced on the radio at Aklavik, a number of trappers—white men and Indians both—were on hand to meet the Inspector and offer their services in the manhunt. Mingled with them were eager spectators—Indian women and youngsters, as well as toil-worn housewives who were as adept as their husbands at building cabins and running traplines. They all cheered at the arrival of May and the others. It was an exciting day in their news-starved lives.

Early the following morning, the eight-man party selected earlier by Eames arrived by dog-sled. Among the posse was trapper Noel Verville, who had assisted in the search practically from its beginning and had been present when Johnson shot and killed Mountie Edgar Millen. The Toronto *Daily Star* was to make mention of the bravery of Noel Verville's wife, who remained alone in a cabin forty miles from her nearest neighbour while her husband went to aid in the search.

Later in the day, May took his plane up again and once more looked for the trail of the wanted man. May is reported as having scouted the Bell River area for a distance of twenty-five miles. At first it seemed a futile search. But finally he found it. The broad snowshoe tracks of Albert Johnson first went south, then abruptly turned to continue directly north for seven miles. Elated, May followed. But it was the old story again. The tracks finally led to some hills swept bare of snow by high winds, and there they were lost.

The following day, from the surrounding reaches of the Yukon, armed men continued to arrive at La Pierre House to volunteer for the great chase. It seemed to have developed into a sort of temporary craze, as though no good home should be without a man who had gone forth on the hunt. Excitement without equal gripped the area, and posses spread out far and wide. An outsider might have come to the conclusion that the masses had gathered to repel an invasion by hostile armies, rather than to capture one exhausted, deathly ill, and half-starved man.

Of course, the news of the great manhunt continued to occupy the radio and the press across the country.

On February 16 a party of eleven men, led by Staff Sergeant Hersey, searched the wild areas east of the Eagle River. There they came upon some recently made snowshoes tracks that caused the hearts of all to beat faster. Then the dogs were mushed ahead in pursuit. For several miles the posse went steadily on at a speed that no man on snowshoes could hope to equal, and expectations began to mount. But, as was usually the case when you pursued the trail of Albert Johnson, frustration followed.

For once again a large and wandering caribou herd had come to the assistance of the Rat River Trapper. According to the written police report: "Johnson managed to take advantage of the caribou tracks. He removed his snowshoes and hiked in the tracks till his trail was lost."

A puzzled party of eleven manhunters made camp that night ten miles north of the Eagle River.

And at the same hour, twenty miles away, another posse of five men were enjoying the warmth of their own campfire before wrapping up in their sleeping blankets after a long day of searching. As they sat there, the sixth member of their party strode from the darkness to the fire and sat down in wordless silence.

He was none other than the noted Indian tracker, Charlie Rat—the same Indian who had led the Eames party to Johnson's cabin. When he was trailing a man, Charlie Rat preferred to be by himself. He had left the posse early that morning to travel alone.

Knowing Charlie Rat, the possemen allowed several minutes to pass before one of them asked:

"Have any luck today, Charlie? Come upon anything interesting?"

"I did. I followed the trail of Albert Johnson, which I finally lost, but I learned many things."

"Such as?"

"I learned that the capture of Albert Johnson is but a matter of a few days. That even if we don't get him there is one who surely will."

Charlie Rat paused to toss a broken twig onto the fire before him.

"In the snow I have seen the long and strong strides of Albert Johnson as they were when the search began, more than forty days ago. But now his footsteps are short and slow, and he often stops to rest. His trail tells the story. I found the deep impressions of his rifle butt in the snow. He has had to lean heavily upon the barrel for support. Once there were the traces that showed that he had sunk to his knees in weakness, and twice I came upon the crimson spots where he had spat blood on the snow."

Slowly Charlie Rat sent his gaze around the listening men in the glow of the campfire.

"So there is no need for us to hurry. He will not go far. Nor do we have long to wait. Three, four, or five days at the most. Death rides on the shoulders of Albert Johnson and is becoming heavier with every step he takes."

CHAPTER NINETEEN

That large posse of Mounties charged on me.
So I shouted, "I'll stay where I am,
And if you cops are looking for trouble
Then you sure have come to the right man."

In the Thursday, February 18, 1932, issue of the
Toronto *Star:*

MOUNTIES SHOOT TO DEATH
MAD TRAPPER OF ARCTIC

———

Johnson Dies Fighting

———

"Edmonton, Feb. 18—Shooting as he dropped,
Albert Johnson, Arctic killer, was literally cut to
pieces in a hail of lead from the guns of a Royal
Canadian Mounted Police posse, Wednesday, when he
was finally cornered in the Eagle River district of the
lonely Yukon. Johnson died after a spectacular battle
as Capt. W. R. "Wop" May winged his way overhead,
waiting for an opportunity to drop bombs on him.
The posse was too close, however, and there was
danger of over-shooting the mark and injuring the
police.

"Johnson's end came suddenly and dramatically.

"For weeks police posses had been following his trail. Johnson's cunning kept him from capture since December 31. Time after time the police found that his trail doubled back and forth. Often he went over hills swept bare of snow so that his trail would be broken.

"Then on Wednesday they at last came upon him and a desperate battle followed, while "Wop" May flew back and forth over the scene in his plane and added to the noise of the miniature war."

Shortly after 7:00 on the morning of Wednesday, February 17, 1932, when Johnson opened his eyes and rose from his sleeping blankets, he was some ten miles east of the Eagle River.

The Rat River Trapper was still travelling under the delusion that the R.C.M.P. were many miles behind him. They might even be unaware that he was now in Yukon Territory with only 170 more miles to go before reaching the Alaska border. And freedom.

In the enshrouding Arctic darkness that somehow always seems to be at its blackest just before daybreak, his groping hands searched for and found the trail-pack he had used for a pillow. Finally he found the small box, removed two kidney pills, and then dropped them into his mouth. The pills would not only serve his medicinal needs, they would likewise have to count as his breakfast. A groan escaped him. Those damnable pains that kept shooting up and down his back.

In the darkness, beside the brush patch where he had spent the previous night, he made ready for another long and tortuous day of trail-travel. His pack was strapped to his shoulders along with the shotgun and the Winchester rifle.

Then, as his mittened right hand picked up his favourite weapon, he heard the familiar sound of the wind—his old friend the whispering wind that came from the Arctic Ocean and seemed to reassure him that all would be well and his trail unimpeded. It was a good omen to start the day. Strong winds could cause violent snow-swirls. Violent snow-swirls could soon obliterate telltale footprints.

Who knows? This could be a lucky day.

To begin with, it stood to reason that with any kind of progress, despite his weakened condition, he could cover a number of miles before the coming of night. There was no reason for any more needless delays. He was far enough ahead of the police by now that time-consuming circling and back-tracking were unnecessary. From now on it would be a direct march westward.

Again, there was that thought which in itself gave him strength to go on.

If all went well and there was still no evidence of any pursuit, he would knock over a caribou or some such succulent game. He would find a deep ravine or gully—one that could conceal any betraying flame. And there, in safety and before the glow of a campfire, he would enjoy the first warmth and hot meal that he had known in nine days. And hot tea before turning in.

He had been on the trail for several hours, making his trudging advance, when behind him he saw the first faint beams of light streaming across the eastern sky. Dawn was coming.

What followed was told by his tracks, which were later found in the snow.

It would appear that around daybreak he paused to rest on a high hill for at least half an hour while around him the world began to lighten and he could study his surroundings. Travelling in the darkness had been a matter of instinct and speculation, but now as the landscape became brighter there was no further need of guesswork.

In all directions there was but a repetition of the scenery he had known for so many days. North, south, east, and west were the long and seemingly endless plains of snow, the occasional mounds of hills and valleys, the odd ravine, and patches of leafless timber whose slender trunks offered little in the way of shelter. Miles upon miles of wind-swept desolation that appeared to have been forgotten by the Almighty. But, having made his observations, Johnson descended the hill, satisfied that the route he had chosen was both the safest and most direct to get him to his destination. Once again he resumed the trek westward.

It was close to 11:30 a.m. when he reached and halted on the east bank of the bleak, narrow Eagle River. He heard the wailing of the wind that seemed to be following directly along the river's course as it continued southward. He saw the clouds of fine snow swirling and slowly settling.

For the present all seemed safe, all seemed serene, with no sound reaching him other than that of the wailing wind. So, removing his snowshoes, he descended the bank and walked to the centre of the frozen river, which was approximately a hundred yards wide at that point. And there, fifty yards ahead, he could see a bend in the river that sharply turned westward. Its course went in the exact direction he was going.

Gladly and unhesitantly he went forward, his snowshoes attached to the two guns, which in turn were strapped to the pack on his shoulders. He still wore his black fur hat. His right hand carried his favourite rifle. His rising hopes seemed to bring new strength as he swiftly rounded the bend in the river and faced west.

But what he beheld there brought him to a sharp halt. For an instant he doubted his own eyes, but the reality was in front of him and it dashed away all hopes of escape, as a life-giving cup is torn from the lips of a dying man.

Less than three hundred yards away, advancing rapidly, was the eleven-man police posse led by Staff Sergeant Hersey of the Mounties.

The oncoming party had seen and recognized the notorious fugitive the same instant his own eyes had fallen upon them. Shouts rang out and dog-teams were jerked to a sudden stop as men grabbed their rifles, ready for battle. For, by now, all of them were well aware that the slightest hesitation could cost them their lives.

"It's Johnson! Shoot! Shoot! Shoot!"

Staff Sergeant Hersey, driving the lead team, was first to fire. Trapper Noel Verville, driving the second team, responded with equal speed. He checked his team and hurried forward to fire beside Hersey. The others ran up beside them.

And Albert Johnson? The truth would seem to be that he was unable to believe the scene before him. Less than a minute earlier he had been certain that any and all trouble from the police was far behind him. That he was well on his way to Alaska.

And now this? This? For several seconds he had been too amazed to do other than gape in incredulity while his dreams and plans crashed around him.

Then came the change. The green eyes narrowed. As the bullets of Hersey and Verville buzzed past his head, he shouted out in a voice that could be heard by every man of the posse:

"You're looking for trouble, and you've come to the right man. I'll give you all the trouble you want. I'll make you sons of bitches wish that you were never born!"

With a movement almost too fast to follow, the hungry gun was whipped up and flashed forward. Two shots rang out in quick succession.

He had fired from a distance of nearly three hundred yards.

His first bullet tore into the chest of Hersey as the latter, with raised rifle, prepared to fire again. The rifle fell from his hands, his eyes glazed. Then he sank to his knees and dropped face forward into the snow, mortally wounded.

The second bullet plunged into the kneecap of trapper Verville, who crumbled to the snow, writhing in agony.

Albert Johnson turned and ran back along the frozen river, around the bend. He dashed back in his own footsteps as desperation lent wings to his heels—the same trail he had made scant minutes earlier. For the first time in his life he had been obliged to retreat before the Mounties. Yet he was no fool. Two members of the posse had fallen, but nine men still remained. All of them were undoubtedly crack shots or they would not have been with that patrol.

And there was method in his retreat. When he had descended the bank to the frozen Eagle River, he had noticed that there was also another course in the winding river fifty yards to the south, also bending sharply westward. It was with the purpose of reaching the southern bend that he was now hurrying, for he realized that, half-concealed in the shelter of the southern bend, it would be a simple matter to pick off, one by one, every last man as they charged around the northern bend of the river a hundred yards away.

They would be coming on fast, expecting no resistance. Yes, and he could drop the lot of them. Every man.

However, there was one problem he was unaware of. Advancing up the southern course of the river was the six-man party that included Charlie Rat. They had heard the sounds of gunfire and guessed its meaning. So it came about that, as he rounded the river bend with a rush, he plunged full into the view of the oncoming patrol. Their rifles instantly swung forward.

He needed only one glance to realize he had run into the path of another police posse. The next instant he wheeled, dashed off on flying feet, again rounded the bend, and disappeared.

Once more the harrowed man ran back in his own footsteps, then halted abruptly midway between the two turns in the river. Now he was in for it. Now the police were coming at him from both ways. He could hear the yells and noise that announced their advance. In a matter of sixty seconds at the most, they would be streaming around both bends in the river while he stood in its centre, an open target.

With the instinct of the wilderness strong within him—the instinct that decrees you must battle till the last—wildly his gaze swept around as he sought at least a temporary shelter where he could make his last stand.

At that instant he heard an ominous droning overhead, the plane of Captain May. As he reached the Eagle River, May began a series of circles that showed he was aware of the grim scene below. His story appeared on the front page of the February 19 issue of the Toronto *Globe:*

EYE WITNESS TELLS HOW MAD TRAPPER MADE LAST STAND.

Captain May is reported to have said: "Aloft, I witnessed the entire battle. Cut off from all avenues of escape, Albert Johnson fought to the very end of his life behind a rock, before he was finally cut to pieces by bullets of the Royal Canadian Mounted Police. Johnson's courage was magnificent."

But as Albert Johnson stood on the frozen river, watching the approaching plane while the sounds of the two oncoming posses got even closer, it was instinct that directed him. Instinct, that spoke to him.

The rock. The rock directly before your eyes at the top of the bank. The spot where you paused to rest before descending to the river. You see it?

Mechanically he nodded.

Then make a bolt for it, Albert Johnson, and hurry. Fight them from behind the rock. They'll be here in thirty seconds and it's your only hope, so hurry. Hurry. And don't lose your head, Johnson. Don't lose your head.

Throwing caution to the wind, he charged across the river to its bank and scaled the ten-foot height with the agility of desperation.

But the effort seemed to have suddenly drained his
remaining strength, and he scarcely had time to
unbuckle his trail-pack before the possemen rounded
both bends in the river. Almost immediately their
sharp eyes found him and a ragged volley rang out.
However, the Rat River Trapper had been that important second faster, and he dropped behind the
shelter of the rock. Then, from one side of it, his rifle
announced that he was ready.

The battle was on.

The press was to say later that the danger of
over-shooting his mark and injuring the police
prevented May from releasing the bombs he carried.
But the members of the posse had been quick to
notice the advantages of their position. The bank
nearest to them, on the west side of the river, was
twice the height of the ten-foot elevation where the
fugitive had taken refuge.

Orders were shouted. With eleven men sprawled in
the snow maintaining the steady rifle fire which
would not permit any reply from Johnson, four men
scaled the west bank. Presently, safely crouched
behind brush and timber, the four—two Mounties and
two trappers—were firing down on the rock a
hundred yards away that sheltered the now helpless
man.

Any attempt on his part to rise up and fire back
was met by a hail of lead from fifteen guns. He was
forced to flatten himself on the snow while hot
pellets of death buzzed around him like angry
hornets. The few shots he did manage to get off were
fired with the haste that made aim impossible. A
bullet sent his black hat flying off his head. Another
tore into his left shoulder.

He shot a glance to the plane overhead and made as though to fire upward. Then, realizing the futility of such an act, he again gave his full attention to the posse.

It is said that once during the battle Albert Johnson shouted out to his attackers, "Why don't you come at me one at a time?"

The steady fusillade went on, and Johnson continued to fire back. At no time did he show the slightest sign of fear, the slightest desire to surrender. He fought to the last. When a bullet shattered his right forearm, he reloaded his rifle and transferred it to his left hand. He could hear the posse members shouting to each other that he had been hit. That he was badly wounded and bleeding.

From the left side of the rock he sent a shot to prove he was still capable of pulling a trigger. He was still dangerous.

Fifteen minutes passed.

By then six possemen had stealthily gained the east bank of the river. There, taking advantage of brush and snow mounds, they crawled slowly to the rear of the rock. Then, from the safety of several small hillocks, they opened up with devastating fire.

Bullet after bullet tore into Albert Johnson. His rifle fell to the snow. His hands were sticky with hot blood.

Captain May was to tell the press:

"Overhead, I could observe that Johnson was flattened on the snow behind the rock as lead came at him from all directions. I could see the snow shoot up all around him when the bullets of the posse missed their mark. I could see his body bounce up and writhe when he was hit. But he fought on till he could no longer lift his gun."

It was all over. Suddenly there was silence. No more flying lead, no more roaring rifles. For it gradually became apparent to the six men to the rear of the rock that the sprawled figure at its base was still.

They rose to their feet, cast glances at each other, then came slowly and cautiously forward with their rifles before them. One beckoned to the other men, who likewise left their positions. Presently, in a wide circle, the fifteen men, rifles at the ready, were advancing upon the figure in the snow. Ten paces from the body the circle halted.

There was no evidence of jubilation or shouts of triumph. None of that.

Instead, an eerie stillness, broken only by the noise of the plane overhead. A stillness during which that hardy and determined fifteen regarded the one before them. And somehow, when the terror of the Arctic lay at their feet, it was a solemn moment. Awed, reluctant, they were paying silent respect to a raw courage the like of which they had never seen.

And as they stood there, the whispering wind mourned a gentle requiem as it drifted over his body.

CHAPTER TWENTY

I fought on to the end and died fighting.
My many wounds reddened the snow.
But just who was the Rat River Trapper?
From my grave, I say no man will know.

The dead body of Albert Johnson was flown back to Aklavik for examination.

All of Albert Johnson's effects were gathered up and checked. Twenty-, fifty-, and hundred-dollar bills in Canadian currency to a total of $2,410 were found on his corpse, along with two American fives and one ten. One of the two small glass jars found in his trail-pack held five pearls. And the other jar contained the seven gold pieces of dental work. This last was to cause much comment and advance the theory that the Mad Trapper of Rat River might have been a mass murderer.

A small box in his pack held thirty-two kidney pills.

No written matter or correspondence of any kind was found either on Albert Johnson's body or in his cabin. If he was having or ever did have any communication with the outside world, there is no evidence of it.

The firearms in his possession were his 99 Savage
.30-30 rifle, his Winchester rifle, and his sawed-off
16-gauge shotgun. His supply of ammunition for his
guns consisted of 127 shells.

A physical description of Albert Johnson at the
time of his death was supplied by Surgeon J. A.
Urquhart of the All Saints Mission at Aklavik.
Surgeon Urquhart listed the dead man's height at 5
feet 10 inches. His weight was placed at 145 pounds.
This would have been thirty pounds less than his
usual weight, and gave mute evidence of the night-
marish ordeal the fugitive had undergone during his
long flight. Trappers who had known him in former
years said, after viewing his dead body, that Albert
Johnson was almost beyond recognition.

A picture of him taken after death shows gaunt
and ghastly features stamped with the agonies of hell.

The corpse had thick brown hair and green eyes.
The only mark on the body, with the exception of
the recently inflicted bullet holes, was a small mole
two inches to the left of the spine in the mid lumbar
region. Surgeon Urquhart set Albert Johnson's age at
between thirty-five and forty.

But just who was the man that the Arctic knew
only as Albert Johnson? Prior to his appearance at
Ross River Post in Yukon Territory on that August
day in 1927, he has no identity.

To be sure, many stories were told of his being
seen prior to that date in various sections of Alaska,
the Yukon, the Northwest Territories, and British
Columbia, as well as elsewhere throughout North
America. And some of the stories could be true. But
none of them was ever confirmed. A check of his
fingerprints did reveal that he had no criminal record.

Since that distant day when Albert Johnson met his death on the frozen Eagle River, over the years, numerous letters from persons in all parts of the world who claimed to be relatives of the Rat River Trapper have been received at the headquarters of the Royal Canadian Mounted Police in Ottawa. In each case the police have patiently checked the contents of the letters, as well as the photos and descriptions that accompanied most of them. But they have always been obliged to reply:

"We find that your claims are not identical with the man known as Albert Johnson."

The story of Albert Johnson's last stand remains an epic of courage almost beyond belief. No matter what else he might have been, he had without question a bravery so utterly contemptuous of death as to be awesome.

If you enjoyed this book
you will enjoy
other

PaperJacks

A division of
General Publishing Co. Limited
Don Mills, Ontario

•

Some of the numerous titles
available in PaperJacks
are described
on the following pages.

PaperJacks

"RUN INDIAN RUN"
Thomas P. Kelley

In June 1906 two of the toughest unhanged rogues in the British Columbia interior were found murdered the day after a drunken brawl at Two-Mile House, near the frontier community of Hazelton. When Simon Gun-an-noot learned that he would be charged with the killings, he took to the woods — knowing that he was innocent and equally certain that he would never get justice in the white man's court. For thirteen years he eluded police posses that were repeatedly sent out after him, and this is the saga of his martyrdom — the deeply moving story of an heroic member of the Kispiox tribe.

$1.50

"ONCE UPON AN ISLAND"
David Conover

Longing to get away from the pressures of city life, the Conovers bought an island off the coast of British Columbia, to develop it into a small resort. This is the story of their earnest but amateurish efforts at plumbing, carpentry, and building, narrow escapes from tragedy, and grim financial struggles — told sensitively and with humour. A real Robinson Crusoe saga — the adventures of a couple that made a dream come true. **$1.50**

PaperJacks

PaperJacks

"THE SECRET OF JALNA"
Ronald Hambleton

What is the secret of Jalna? Did a house called Jalna really exist? Who was Mazo de la Roche and why did she hide her origins? What kept the Jalna stories off television for ten years after her death? Ronald Hambleton explores the mysteries surrounding Mazo de la Roche, her family, and the Whiteoaks. With 122 illustrations including the Whiteoak family tree.

$1.95

"FRED DALE'S GARDEN BOOK"
H. Fred Dale

Canada's newest gardening guide, with easy, step-by-step instructions that make it possible for home owners to grasp instantly the techniques that will result in beautiful lawns and gardens. This handy book has five sections covering lawns, the summer garden, woody plants, hardy bulbs, and a wide range of growing problems — growing in shade, preparing for vacation, pruning, making compost, and dealing with plant pests. Through his columns in the *Toronto Star* and *Canadian Homes* Fred Dale is in touch with more Canadian gardeners than any other writer. **$1.95**

"YOUR NAME AND COAT-OF-ARMS"
The Rev. James S. McGivern, S.J.

This book explains the origin and gives some of the intriguing history behind hundreds of our most frequently occurring family names. Some 1,250 surnames common in Canada are indexed, and for many of them the book shows the crests and coats-of-arms traditionally associated with the names. **$1.50**

PaperJacks

CANADIAN CRITICAL ISSUES SERIES
Edited by John A. Eisenberg and Malcolm A. Levin

"Foreign Ownership"

American ownership of Canadian businesses — unquestionably a problem of paramount importance in our country today. Examine several detailed case studies that illustrate the nature and extent of foreign ownership, the inherent limitations of "branch plant" operations, and the conflicts between U.S. and Canadian trade policies. Where do you stand on this question? **$1.25**

"The Law and the Police"

When individual rights are infringed in the course of law enforcement, controversy inevitably arises. Recent examples of this are explored here, involving the use of force by police, the invasion of the privacy of suspected criminals, and the granting of special powers to the police by the War Measures Act. **$1.25**

"Don't Teach That!"

Who has the right to teach matters of personal belief? Governments often introduce programs for teaching sex, religion, politics, and morals in the schools. Parents protest, claiming it is their responsibility within the family. Read this probing inquiry into a widely debated question. **$1.25**

"Rights of Youth"

Current unrest in our schools is scrutinized in the light of recent actual cases of conflict involving students, parents, and school authorities. The practical role of the school in society, the status of youth in the schools, the thin line between parental and school authority, and the degree of freedom a student should have at school — these are the issues. **$1.25**

PaperJacks

"DRUGS, SOCIETY AND PERSONAL CHOICE"
Drs. Harold and Oriana Kalant

This book aims to put into the sharpest possible focus questions of fact and matters of value judgment, and how the two interact. The authors' purpose is to encourage the type of discussion that the LeDain Commission has requested and that the subject fully deserves. Both authors are associated with the Addiction Research Foundation in Toronto. **$1.95**

"THE PURSUIT OF INTOXICATION"
Dr. Andrew I. Malcolm

This book examines the many reasons why people have used and continue to use the psychoactive drugs. These are considered under five main headings: religion, medicine, endurance, extinction, and recreation. Dr. Malcolm also touches on his theory regarding the alienating influence of such illusionogenic drugs as marihuana and LSD. **$2.50**

"THE FORGOTTEN CHILDREN"
R. Margaret Cork

"Dad's spoiled every Christmas I can remember because he smashes the tree . . ." So says 14-year-old Jean, one of the "Forgotten Children". Charles, at 15, puts his mother to bed when she's drunk. Sharon has survived to age 11 with two alcoholic parents. These and 100 other voices of 10- to 16-year-olds are not those of the "needy and poor" in our society. Yet their need is desperate. **95 cents**

PaperJacks

"THE TRUDEAU QUESTION"
W. A. Wilson

Pierre Elliott Trudeau: the man, his politics, his background, his wife, his public, his record, his holidays, his future – all part of *The Trudeau Question*, an exclusive, controversial report by the Ottawa editor of the Montreal *Star*. Featuring a pictorial account of Trudeau's administration, charts tracing Trudeau's record on unemployment, popularity, etc., and a guide to election-watching. $2.95

"THE INCREDIBLE JOURNEY"
Sheila Burnford

The world-famous story of three animals who walked home. There was Luath, a young and gentle Labrador with a red-gold coat and a noble head. There was Tao, the hunter, a sleek wheat-coloured Siamese cat. And there was Bodger, the old half-blind Bull Terrier, with a strong sense of humour. The three animals walked and ran, fought and struggled together, escaped death at almost every step, and finally came home as though they could never again be parted from the dream of their incredible journey.
75 cents

PaperJacks

"TO UNDERSTAND JEWS"
Stuart E. Rosenberg

This book clarifies Jewish views on immortality, sex, sin, marriage, the "chosenness" of the Jewish people, the Messiah, and other significant points. It describes the evolution of Jewish culture and religion from biblical times to the present. It tells the story of the gallant struggle of a people for survival, and of the religion and culture that sustained them. Its simple eloquence rips through the veils of ignorance and misunderstanding and opens the way towards one of man's noblest goals: the recognition of human brotherhood. $1.25

"THE SACRED MUSHROOM AND THE CROSS"
John M. Allegro

A major breakthrough in our understanding of the origin and nature of the languages of the Bible has made possible the decipherment of the names of the Jewish God and the patriarchs, and now shows the religion of the Israelites and their inheritors, the Christians, to have been founded in a very ancient fertility cult centred on the worship of the sacred mushroom, the red-topped *Amanita muscaria*. $1.50.

PaperJacks

"GROOKS"
Piet Hein

Grook-writing is just one dimension of Piet Hein's creative life. He is the "compleat creator", not subject to the schizoid art versus science malady of modern times. The inventor of Grooks is also the author of the superellipse – the "rectangular oval" used in the new Stockholm city centre, a delight of mathematical art. "The impact of Piet Hein ... on the English speaking world may be considerable ... he comes to its attention as a fullblown, developed genius ..." *Life*. Volumes I, II, III – each $1.25

"THE MORTALITY MERCHANTS"
G. Scott Reynolds

The legalized racket of life insurance and what you can do about it. The millions of Canadian holders of life insurance policies will find this book a shocking revelation of the financial trap into which most of them have fallen. The author argues that the enormous complexities of life insurance exist for a single purpose – to keep the buyer off balance and in a state of confusion. He discloses fully exactly what life insurance is, what it can and cannot do, and how the basic function of the industry has been all but forgotten. $1.50

PaperJacks